NO VACANCY:
Homeless Women in Paradise

NO VACANCY:
Homeless Women in Paradise

Michael E. Reid

Introduction by Dan Baldwin

2LEAF PRESS

NEW YORK

www.2leafpress.org

P.O. Box 4378
Grand Central Station
New York, New York 10163-4378
editor@2leafpress.org
www.2leafpress.org

2LEAF PRESS
is an imprint of the
Intercultural Alliance of Artists & Scholars, Inc. (IAAS),
a NY-based nonprofit 501(c)(3) organization that promotes
multicultural literature and literacy.
www.theiaas.org

Cover photo and design: Donna Murphy
Copy editor: Carolina Fung Feng
Book design and layout: Gabrielle David

Library of Congress Control Number: 2017963100

ISBN-13: 978-1-940939-71-1 (Paperback)
ISBN-13: 978-1-940939-81-0 (eBook)

10   9   8   7   6   5   4   3   2   1

Published in the United States of America

First Edition | First Printing

2Leaf Press trade distribution is handled by University of Chicago Press /
Chicago Distribution Center (www.press.uchicago.edu) 773.702.7010. Titles are
also available for corporate, premium, and special sales. Please direct inquiries
to the UCP Sales Department, 773.702.7248.

All proceeds received by the author for the sale of this book will be donated to the Fund for Homeless Women at the Community Foundation for Monterey County in support of programs and services for women who are homeless in Monterey County.

But nothing can be changed
Until it is faced

—James Baldwin

CONTENTS

✣ ✣ ✣ ✣

PREFACE | V

ACKNOWLEDGMENTS | IX

INTRODUCTION | 1

ONE
THE DISCOVERY | 7

TWO
TO SEE WITH NEW EYES | 17

THREE
A TRIBE EXHUMED | 21

FOUR
THE COLD HARD FACTS | 27

FIVE
PREPARATION FOR SERVICE |
33

SIX
SECRETS OF THE DEAD | 39

SEVEN
PEELING THE ONION | 43

EIGHT
BECOMING VISIBLE | 51

NINE
FILLING THE GAPS | 59

TEN
THE THREE AMIGOS | 65

ELEVEN
EMPTY NESTERS | 73

TWELVE
NOW WHAT? | 81

THIRTEEN
FINDING OUR WAY | 89

FOURTEEN
NEIGHBORHOODS | 99

FIFTEEN
A NATURAL WOMAN | 109

SIXTEEN
STORIES OF TRANSFORMATION | 123

SEVENTEEN
DEPRESSION | 133

EIGHTEEN
LETTING GO | 139

NINETEEN
SHAME | 149

TWENTY
THE STORY CONTINUES | 155

EPILOGUE | 157
ABOUT THE AUTHOR | 163
OTHER BOOKS BY 2LEAF PRESS | 165

PREFACE

✛ ✛ ✛ ✛

WHEN I RECEIVED A LETTER from a stranger alerting me to the hundreds of women living without shelter in one of the most affluent sea-side communities in California, and the dead bodies being found in plain sight, I was compelled to act on their behalf. Having suffered from alienation as a black, gay Episcopal priest, I quickly identified with these women, so I asked two of my friends (one Buddhist, the other Jewish) to join me on a quest to make a difference in our community and in the lives of women living without shelter. Over the course of the next five years, together with the Community Foundation for Monterey County (CFMC), we formed the Fund for Homeless Women, mobilized a community, raised public awareness, secured venture capital instrumental in opening five new programs specifically designed to address the needs of this unique and quickly growing population, and started an endowment, making the invisible visible for generations yet to come.

I was moved to write *No Vacancy* because I wanted to share my incredible journey—from discovering this hidden secret on the Central Coast of California, to uncovering the complicated reasons for its existence, and being challenged by the barriers that prevent its amelioration—even in the place many call "paradise." In it you will read stories of women both dead and alive that will surprise you, challenge your notions of the homeless, and take you on the circuitous road of grassroots social change. This is especially relevant today as communities face weakened political will, dwindling financial support from the government and unreliable measures for social justice. In the United States, we all live with the growing reality of homelessness, even in places where you least expect it. But ultimately, each one of us can make a difference, find purpose, a place to belong and a way out of whatever shadows that compromise our ability to dream and act for the greater good—for causes once thought to be outside of ourselves. In that regard, *No Vacancy* is as much these women's stories as it is mine.

It would be wonderful if you would come away with a better understanding of the issues contributing to homelessness in the United States, and particularly in communities like the Monterey Peninsula in California. Perhaps you will see how we are all complicit in one way or another, and find your own mobilization for change. With these stories of homeless women we have encountered, I hope you will recognize and come to know the people in these circumstances as neighbors and friends, just like you.

Along the way you may be surprised by what you find in these pages and by what you discover in yourself.

Hopefully, any perceptions and assumptions you may have had about people who are homeless will be challenged or even transformed. Starting with the discovery of death, I hope that you will discover life, and see how all our lives come together like mosaics in a colorful work of art.

But be prepared; like life, this is not a linear journey. Although there is a definite chronology, this is not a conventional narrative. My reflection offers waves of memory not always related to time. One event connected me to another, like the process of building answers to a question not fully formed. It has been and continues to be an active process. As with all of us—who come from different places, we move in a similar direction, need the same things and remind each other of how much we have and how easily it can all be lost.

Thank you for your interest in this book. It is my hope that you will allow yourself to be taken on a journey. In the end, I hope you will begin to see women who are homeless with new eyes. If I have been successful, you might also be challenged to see yourself and the people around you differently, more critically, behind the facade, and to consider the complexities and contradictions in all our lives.

Each of us has the power to make a difference in our lives and in the lives of others—to become our best selves individually, and in community. Here is my random attempt to create change in myself and in the world around me. May it inspire you. I believe that is exactly what we are all on this earth to do.◙

—Michael E. Reid

ACKNOWLEDGMENTS

✝ ✝ ✝ ✝

I BELIEVE WE ARE ALL interconnected and interdependent. Nothing worthwhile is accomplished without the support or involvement of others. And in the case of *No Vacancy*—there are many others, known and unknown who have played an important role in the authoring of this book. Actually, far too many to mention here, but several who must be given special mention.

First and foremost, I acknowledge Joyce—the woman whose strength, courage and determination brought the issues of homeless women to my attention and who invited me into a world I barely knew existed. It is due to her and the countless women who live in danger without adequate shelter that I have dedicated my efforts on behalf of homeless women, which ultimately led to this book. In that vein, I also include the individuals who are dedicated to helping homeless women, and who attempt to ameliorate the many pathways to homelessness. With them in partnership, there are also the countless donors, advocates and policy makers—whose generous investments of time, talent or financial resources, make possible the various forms of life-giving support toward housing, safety and self-sufficiency. I sincerely commend you all.

The Fund for Homeless Women and its success in facilitating shelter, safety and community would not have been possible without my colleagues, Kathy Whilden and Marian Penn. They have been essential to my life and to the existence of this important work and the Fund. I also want to especially thank Dan Baldwin, Christine Dawson, staff; and the board of the Community Foundation for Monterey County (CFMC), who looked beyond the challenges and said "yes" to the vision, passion and collective desire to work toward a just and healthier community for all our residents. They took bold steps, and agreed to walk into the fray, and I am forever grateful for our partnership.

Most commendable continues to be my spouse, Bill Robnett, without whom, life as I know it would not be the same, nor would my ability to so completely dedicate myself to the needs of others. My faith and friends—have all taught me how to go into unknown places, to listen and to act with courage and conviction—a process that continues to serve me well.

Michele Crompton, Elin Kelsey, Roxane Buck-Esquella, Patrice Vecchione, Sandy Kanh and others encouraged me to write. Donna Murphy of Rapid Printers, and Gabrielle David of 2Leaf Press, provided a platform and the support to pull it all together. And there are so many others.

It takes a village, and I remain eternally grateful for mine.

Names of women living without adequate shelter have been changed or altered as per their wishes. Stories are printed with their permission.

All proceeds received by the author for the sale of this book will be donated to the Fund for Homeless Women at the Community Foundation for Monterey County in support of programs and services for women who are homeless in Monterey County.

Please join us and consider making a tax-deductible contribution to:

Fund for Homeless Women
Community Foundation for Monterey County
2354 Garden Road
Monterey, CA 93940 ▣

INTRODUCTION

✢ ✢ ✢ ✢

T IS DIFFICULT TO KNOW where to begin, because the narrative of homelessness has so many entry points. There really is not a beginning or a middle, and often the end is indeed that: the end. What we do know is that a combination of factors (job loss, medical conditions, mental illness, addiction, divorce, death of a spouse or partner, rising cost of housing, and many more) have sent homeless numbers skyrocketing across the U.S.

California is "home" to the largest population of the homeless, and it affects all our communities. Beyond the obvious human tragedy of seeing displaced persons living in deplorable conditions, it is a drain on local economies as retail and hospitality centers try to motivate customers to not be deterred by the person sleeping at the bus stop or holding a sign seeking a handout. It is a situation that stresses state and local governments that funnel money to nonprofits who provide services. It erodes confidence in our systems and sense of humanity as we wonder what each of us can do to assist. And it stigmatizes and depicts the homeless as lazy, who only want others to care for them without taking personal responsibility for their circumstances. We have become desensitized to remembering that each one of these people has a story.

Compounding this tragedy is that the folks we see on the street represent a small percentage of our homeless population. Many are sleeping in cars, are couch surfing, living in shelters, or simply stay out of sight. For example, in Monterey County, four families living in a three-bedroom house are not considered homeless. And for all the terrifying and growing numbers connected to homelessness, they do not reflect the equally growing number of those at risk of becoming homeless.

I am not sure I would have met Michael Reid before he came to my office at the Community Foundation for Monterey County (CFMC) to talk about starting the Fund for Homeless Women. In the idiom of community foundations, he was describing a field-of-interest fund, meaning a fund that is defined by a specific purpose, but is not limited to supporting named nonprofit agencies. In this case, the idea was that donors would give into the fund, knowing that grants would support agencies working to intervene on behalf of homeless women (or women at risk of becoming homeless) on the Monterey Peninsula.

While all this sounded well and good—and there was certainly an urgent need—there was one major catch in this plan: there was no money. Michael brought emotion, passion, vision, and fundraising experience, but no gift with which to start the fund. The nomenclature itself describes the dilemma; a fund requires funds.

But it was hard to reject Michael's energy. I believed he could deliver on his pledge to raise considerable resources in support of homeless women. I took the idea to our next meeting of the CFMC board of directors. We are an organization that prides itself on being entrepreneurial, but a fund with no funds? The board was also concerned about possible confusion with the CFMC's well established Women's Fund, which at the time was in the middle of a campaign to grow its endowment. I pushed the board to look beyond these issues, and, not to parody a popular movie, simply said, "There is something about Michael." The fund was approved.

The word-of-mouth network surrounding local philanthropic initiatives never fails to surprise. One of our then newer donor advisors (community foundations hold many donor-advised funds, grantmaking "accounts" out of which donors recommend grants) had learned of the newly established Fund for Homeless Women. This particular donor-advised fund is anonymous. They recommended a grant of $50,000. A few days later Michael came to our offices for a scheduled meeting with our Vice President for Philanthropic Resources. Her office is next door to mine. A minute or two after he entered, I heard a big "WHOOP." His vision was being rewarded.

No Vacancy describes Michael's journey, which is appropriate, because solving homelessness, even for one individual, is also a journey. It requires considerable social infrastructure that include nonprofits, case managers, substance abuse and/or mental health treatment, transitional and affordable housing, family support, personal will and the desire to change circumstances. It also requires resources. Lots of resources. Federal, state, county, local and philanthropic. It requires people who care, who are willing to act, and who are willing to motivate others to do the same.

Data is important, but it can also be dehumanizing, especially when numbers are so staggering. We can choose to step around our homeless, or simply walk away, but doing so only exacerbates a growing human and economic tragedy. When confronted with a real person, a single human circumstance that had ended badly, Michael Reid chose to stop, observe, feel and act. Now, thankfully, many others are following in his footsteps.◙

—Dan Baldwin
President/CEO
Community Foundation for Monterey County

ONE

✢ ✢ ✢ ✢

THE DISCOVERY

A DECOMPOSED BODY was found in a large open field adjacent to the Barnyard Shopping Center in Carmel, California. It's a large open lot behind the Chevron gas station on the corner of Rio Road and Highway One. This horrific discovery was mentioned briefly in the Monterey County Herald without mention of gender or the circumstances related to the death. The case was under investigation.

The next day, among stories about Donald Trump, the local traffic, lost dogs and monarch butterflies, there was a brief announcement that the body found the day before was that of a woman. Her identity and age were unknown. The cause of her death was called "suspicious," and the area where they found her body was identified as one frequented by "transients." Nothing more was reported.

I thought back to six years prior when a woman was raped on the grounds of my church in Pacific Grove. I came to work one morning, and discovered a young woman claiming to have been raped the night before while sleeping outside on the church steps. Participants in a twenty-year-old program for homeless men had been sleeping inside the parish hall, and she said that at some point in the early hours of the morning, one of the men came out and raped her.

For several days prior, I and others at the church had attempted to find a place for her to be housed. She had been given and used several nights of hotel vouchers, after calling all the numbers we could find for service providers and possible shelter. Yet nowhere was there a place for her to find a bed and adequate safety.

She was too old for youth programs. She didn't have children; was not mentally ill, drug addicted or escaping an abusive partner. She was unemployed, evicted from her home, and now, not meeting the criteria for the few shelters on the Monterey Peninsula, was relegated to living outside. After receiving food, clothing, blankets and a sleeping bag, she decided to sleep on the church steps. She said that was where she had felt safest.

Through tears she told me her frightening story. I called the police. They quickly arrived, as did a team of reporters with cameras from the local news stations. She was taken to the hospital and after alleging rape, finally qualified for emergency housing. Because she had become a victim of a violent crime, she now met the needed criteria.

My friend Kathy told me that there was a huge backlog for the actual review of rape kits. We imagined hundreds of kits lined up and forgotten on a warehouse shelf. Although this young woman was reportedly given a medical examination, little if anything might have been done to study her most recent addition of swabs, fluids and hair. We hoped that this case would be looked into, allegations reviewed, the rapist found. But we heard nothing more of the investigation. It seemed as if the incident was going to go cold. As far as we knew, it had, along with hundreds of others. Evidence silenced and cases unsolved, perhaps forever.

The dead nameless woman discovered in Carmel reminded me of this shameful allegation of rape. This body was the third to be found dead in the open on the Monterey Peninsula, or at least it was the third incident that I had heard about. There were probably many more.

The prior year, a homeless woman was found dead in the lake of a park in my Monterey neighborhood—a new bird sanctuary now run by the Audubon Society. Those who cared stood in shock and disbelief on the bridge above the place her body was found. In silence, we reflected on the gruesome tragedy that occurred right beneath our feet.

Her name was Charlene. She was in her fifties, a veteran with PTSD who was devastated by the death of her former husband. She had been laid off twice and unable to find a job. After eviction and couch surfing, Charlene resorted to a tent in the park, and soon afterward was discovered face down in the lake.

The year before, a woman was found dead behind the Carmel Women's Club. An impromptu requiem was offered at Church of the Wayfarer. Some members of the community gathered and shared their memories of encountering her walking back and forth on Ocean Avenue, or reading in the Carmel Public Library. She too was homeless. Very few passersby had known her name. Rumor was that she had once been a librarian—aged out of the system and priced out of her home. Although not a member of the Women's Club, she died as close to it as she could possibly get.

Three women found dead of suspicious causes on the Monterey Peninsula, broken bodies decomposing in the open, and still nothing but a few printed words to mark their humiliating demise in a place so many call "paradise."

With the memory of the young woman claiming to have been raped on the church steps, this newest discovery of flesh and bones grew like a heavy weight on me. I couldn't seem to get the thought of these bodies out of my mind. Why weren't more people talking about this? What was being done to find out who they were, how they lived and ultimately died?

Homeless people are three times more likely to die early. The average age of death for a homeless person is about fifty. If you live indoors, you can expect to live almost thirty years longer. Homeless women are especially at risk.

People who are homeless suffer the same illnesses experienced by those with homes, but at rates three to six times higher. This includes diseases such as HIV/AIDS, tuberculosis and influenza, but their deaths also result from cancer, heart disease, diabetes and hypertension.

Unlike what most people may think, the risk of death on the streets is only moderately affected by substance abuse or mental illness. These causes are most often assumed to be the deadliest. But lack of sleep, irregular medication schedules, poor diets, inadequate hygiene and the cold can prolong and exacerbate illnesses, sometimes to the point where they are life threatening.

And then, there's exposure to the elements. Two men died of hypothermia on the streets of Monterrey during the winter of 2016. In the coldest areas of the United States, homeless individuals have an eightfold risk of dying from exposure when compared to those who are housed and warm.

But perhaps worst of all, the homeless also die because of unprovoked violence against them. Ten years ago, there was a documented 472 acts of violence against homeless people by people who are housed around the country, including 169 murders. Today it's even more frequent.

But these facts fail to satisfy. Statistically, the numbers do not match up with the the loss of life that seemed to be accumulating around me. The appearance of complacency caused me to grow angry, and fueled my need to learn more.

Every day I looked in the paper for a follow-up article about this new body discovered out in the open. I looked for public letters of outrage. After seeing none, I wrote a letter of my own and sent it to the editor of the *Monterey Herald.* It read:

> *Another woman is found dead on the Monterey Peninsula (Body found in Carmel is female, August 31, Monterey Herald). Like the woman found in Laguna Grande Park, and the one discovered close to the Carmel Women's Club, this death is being connected to "...transients...", if only because of the open field that served as her grave. We may never know how many more bodies of women have been found, or how many are still waiting to be discovered.*
>
> *We may never know the identity or circumstances of this most recent tragedy, but it is possible that she was one of the more than 500 women who are currently homeless on the peninsula, needing shelter and safety.*
>
> *Once again, the discovery of this woman's body offers our community with a call to provide shelter for those who are forced to sleep outside, and much needed services to help prevent the all too frequent destruction and ultimate loss of human life. No one deserves to be disposed of in such a callous and anonymous way, leaving to our imagination the conditions of her life. We shouldn't just shake our heads in sadness or disbelief. We should do what we can before another woman's body is found broken and dead.*

I emailed the reporter who wrote the article about the nameless woman, to see if he could provide any additional information about the case, or at least advise me on how I might learn more, but he didn't reply. I called him and left a message. He didn't call back.

I reviewed the Carmel police records, called the police station, wrote to the Carmel Chief of Police, read the Carmel newspaper, but found absolutely nothing written about the woman who was left to rot where thousands drive by on their way to dine, shop or visit the natural beauty of the Highlands or Big Sur. There was no information and no public outrage. The sound of apathy was deafening.

Day after beautiful day rolled by (this happens frequently in paradise). While making a presentation about homelessness to a group of teens at the Youth Arts Collective in Monterey, a young female participant suddenly raised her hand and said, "I was homeless." All her friends turned to her in surprise. You could have heard a pin drop. She was young, blonde, pretty, about fifteen years of age. She decided to be fully known.

This brave young woman went on to say that she and her mother had been homeless in Monterey. She didn't explain when or the reason for being without shelter, but told the group that they couldn't find a shelter to accommodate her and her mother, and they had to sleep on the beach for several nights. She said she was cold, hungry and very scared. Finally, a bed in a shelter for families became available and they found their way back to safety and ultimately, housing.

She said she was totally surprised that there were so many other females out there. What she didn't know was that there were at least 500 others, unsheltered and in danger. She was alive. I wondered whose body might be discovered next.

Her friend pulled out the twenty dollars she had earned in babysitting the night before, and made a tearful contribution to my effort.

City Council members seemed to be throwing their hands up. They claimed the problem was too big for the city to handle on its own. Most of the council members believed that homelessness, and the lack of affordable housing was an issue that could only be dealt with by help from the County and the State. It was too big a problem for them to effectively manage or change on their own. After all, 10 percent of the children in the Monterey Unified School District were homeless. That is 900 children on the peninsula alone. What could they be expected to do with 900 children, they asked. What could they do with 500 women? The problem was simply too big.

I couldn't let this go, and sent the reporter a second message:

I wrote to you a few days ago and haven't heard back. As I mentioned in my prior email, I'm interested in learning what is known about the woman whose body was found in Carmel last week. Because of my work with women who are homeless on the Peninsula, I wonder if she was indeed homeless, and what the circumstances were around her death.

Please advise me if you have more information, and/or let me know how I might learn more about this case.

Many thanks. I look forward to hearing from you soon.

After several more days, there was still no reply. I did get a response from the Carmel Chief of Police. He informed me that the case was being handled by the Monterey County Sheriff's Department, and that it was totally out of his hands.

More days came and went. I tried not to obsess. I tried to forget. But I would invariably run into someone on the street who would mention my letter to the editor and thank me for caring and for staying involved. Even if I could eventually let it go, others wouldn't let me. I wrote to the County Sheriff's Office. I called. I wrote again. Nothing.

After what felt like an eternity, the reporter finally called me back. He said that he hadn't learned anything else. He concurred that the case was still under investigation by the Sheriff's office, and they probably couldn't give me any more information. But I wasn't satisfied. I couldn't understand how this could happen.

I wrote the reporter again. I thanked him for getting back to me and for giving me an update. But I went on to tell him that I was a priest involved in a ministry to raise public awareness and support for homeless women, and I was looking for data that would help our community better understand how women without adequate shelter lived and died. I had been familiar with two prior cases. Perhaps there were others that I was unaware of. I asked him to help me, to point me in the direction of statistics and stories related to this issue. I knew it was a long shot, but maybe he cared about this as much as I did. It might actually make a difference in someone's life. ▣

TWO

✛ ✛ ✛ ✛

TO SEE WITH NEW EYES

UNDERSTOOD THE REPORTER'S reluctance, the sense of being overwhelmed, and the apparent apathy of others. I myself didn't always pay such close attention to this issue. It wasn't until I was encouraged to look more deeply that I began to see the problem with new eyes. Although generally concerned about social justice, I had never focused my attention on the homeless or even on women's causes. But it seemed as if all the while, the events of my life were preparing me to finally see more clearly. When it was presented to me I felt ready to step in, to participate in the dilemma, to attempt to make a difference in an area I knew absolutely nothing about.

It all started with a letter I received from a stranger named Joyce. As a parish priest, I received quite a bit of mail—mostly junk. But with no return address to be found, and my full name boldly handwritten across the envelope, I felt that this was not something to be tossed aside or left unopened. Inside was a letter that changed my life. I read every word repeatedly. These are the ones that stuck:

> "...there are too many homeless women in the streets without help...

> When I was homeless I had no family to help me, plus it was during the rainy season and it was getting cold. I had no sleeping bag or blanket, no tent, nothing to protect me...

> ...no safety while sleeping in the open...

> No woman needs to wonder if she will be raped during the night or live to see another day."

She asked if I could help because she felt "invisible." She said that women were being victimized on the beach, raped in parks and under the very freeways we drive over every day.

> "Please help us. We need to be seen before it's too late."

I remember it was the word "invisible" that stopped me cold. It latched on to me and took root. It was like the missing puzzle piece that I had been searching for and finally found.

I too felt invisible. Being black and gay in a majority white heterosexual world, so much of me felt like a ghost. Although standing out in the crowd, I felt unseen and unknown for all that I was. And so did Joyce and her community of women living outside.

Invisible and without voice.

Suddenly I felt a deep kinship with these women living without shelter and safety, many walking past wounded, unnoticed, disguised, traumatized, trying to fit in, to belong, and for their stories to be told, to be heard, recognized for all that they were, to be named before they too were found dead.

I am the firstborn American son of Caribbean immigrants. I have always felt disconnected, unmoored. Moving through expectations, trying to assimilate as much as possible to the majority culture, but never really fitting in, never feeling fully seen; though housed, not really belonging anywhere.

I think most people live with preconceived notions of who everyone else is. Who they are and why they live as they do. We make judgments, compare ourselves to what we see on the facade; rarely discovering the truth that lies within, the reasons why, the journeys taken and what one leaves behind.

To some extent we are all invisible to each other, while wanting desperately to be seen and understood. And so, from the moment I read the letter from Joyce, I was hooked. I found a tribe to which I too could belong and together with them and whoever else I could convince to join me, I was committed to doing what I could. ▣

THREE

✝ ✝ ✝ ✝

A TRIBE EXHUMED

AFTER SEVERAL MORE DAYS of waiting to hear from anyone about the dead body, I received a message from the County Sheriff's office. The Commander apologized for the delay in getting back to me. He went on to say that after checking with the County Coroner they discovered that over the past ten years there had been at least thirty recorded cases of dead women labeled "transient" found in the county. He explained that the number didn't include bodies found outside of the Sheriff's jurisdiction, and noted that there had been a few more bodies recently found that were not included in the number given.

I called him back and explained my interest in learning more. He said that he ran the investigative unit and was currently very busy with arrest warrants. He asked if I would be able to come to his office if I couldn't get the assistance I needed over the phone. "Absolutely!" I said. "I could be there later that day or the next." This was exactly what I was waiting for. My persistence finally seemed to be paying off, and I was given contact information for others in the department who might be able to help me.

While talking, the Commander tried to search for an email thread he and his staff had constructed in response to my initial request. Besides easily uncovering thirty cases of dead women found in his jurisdiction over the past ten years, his investigation also revealed that the woman most recently found in Carmel was indeed homeless. As was the woman just found in Castroville.

"Castroville?" I told him that I hadn't heard about a body being found in Castroville. The last one I heard about (and was responding to) was the one discovered in Carmel. "Yes," he said. "Since the body in Carmel, another woman was found dead. This one in Castroville. She was discovered in a ditch and was believed to have been homeless."

After my contact with the County Sheriff's Department, I called the Deputy in the coroner's office to continue my inquiry. The Deputy remembered speaking with his commander about me. He apologized for his antiquated database system — which was going to be upgraded later that week, but concurred that his search had uncovered thirty cases of dead bodies that were labeled "female homeless."

He said it was difficult to pull statistics because of limitations in the system, and that a good deal of information was not actually coded by gender. He was however, able to verify the information offered, noted anecdotally that there were very few homicides in the homeless community committed by the homeless against each other, and stated that while there was an average of about three bodies of women found each year, he couldn't discern any particular trends.

He said that there may have been more bodies found than were actually noted. Apparently, you have to check the homeless box when filing a report for the body to actually be coded as "homeless." It was possible that in other cases, an officer might have failed to do so.

The Deputy explained that quite a bit of work went into processing these cases. When a body is discovered they are required to first establish identification. DNA, fingerprints and dental records are all used if the person doesn't have a government ID among her belongings. Jail and hospital databases are also used to help identify the discarded dead, and to determine if there are family members listed anywhere as next of kin. And then they try to determine the cause of death.

Of the thirty bodies of women found within the jurisdiction of the County Sheriff's Department since 2006, one died because of cancer, three were suicides, two were homicides. There were eight accidents, twelve died of natural causes, two were undetermined, and two in motor vehicle accidents. Most of the cases were found in Salinas (18), Monterey and Seaside were next (with 3 each). Carmel, Sand City and Pacific Grove followed (with 1 each). This did not include the most recent discovery in Carmel. Her case was still under investigation.

Besides city location, what I found most startling was the age of the women who had been found: 60 percent were fifty-one years of age and older. Thirteen were fifty-one to sixty, two were seventy-one to seventy-five and one was ninety-eight years old.

It was an unusually hot day when I spoke with the Deputy. I thanked him for his service, and (trying to be convivial and to show my appreciation) suggested that he stay cool. He laughed and said that the coroner's office was always kept cool. I asked him if I could call again if I had further questions, and he said, "please do."

And that's just what I needed to hear because there were many questions still left unanswered. We had numbers but still no names. We had data but still no stories.

Who were these women? What were the circumstances of their lives and deaths? What did their personal narratives have to teach us? I wanted to find out. But I didn't know how. There are no obituaries written for homeless women whose bodies are found on the side of the road. To my surprise however, the County Board of Supervisors Public Records Act makes records of such deaths available to the public. And so my journey continued.

I found out that each case cost ten dollars and were available through the County Coroner's office. After asking for more information, the Deputy called back to inform me of the actual process. He suggested I speak to his secretary to make the arrangements, which I immediately did.

I explained to his secretary that I was looking for stories, and that I wanted to know more about these women found dead in our communities. Perhaps there was information in public records that would help me build the narrative arc of their lives.

I was forewarned that all I would find in these documents were reports from the Coroner—information from the autopsy and toxicology screenings. I didn't know how much of a narrative arc I could build, but I thought it was well worth pursuing. So I decided to file the request and paid for ten cases. Delving into one third of the cases would be a good start. It would at least provide a sample of what the others might offer, and bring me another step closer to the truth. Another step closer to putting the lives of these women in full view, and understanding their path to homelessness. ▣

FOUR

✢ ✢ ✢ ✢

THE COLD HARD FACTS

PERHAPS ONE OF THE MOST essential qualities for someone attempting to make a difference or longing to create social change is naïvety. If you know too much, you'll probably never try. I was certainly naïve when I originally launched on this journey to address the needs of women who are homeless. Although I may not have been able to admit it to myself at the time, I didn't have a clue about what I was getting myself into.

Apparently, my personal connection to homeless women and the passion I felt about the mission, outweighed any lack of knowledge and understanding about the complexity of the issue. The systems that created homelessness particularly for women are innumerable, and oftentimes overwhelming. At first I didn't fully understand. Most people who live "inside" do not.

Most of us in America have become aware of the disparity in income between men and women, but in years past and despite having a daughter, I never thought in detail about how such a disparity might actually disadvantage women in hiring and retention practices, savings, retirement, affordability of child care, housing, homelessness, and even death.

Poverty and loss of income are the primary causes of homelessness.

I didn't realize the effects of ageism, and the fact that while women over fifty are the first to be laid off, they are the least likely to be rehired.

Almost 50 percent of homeless women on the Monterey Peninsula are over fifty.

I never considered the ultimate relationship between low income, and the rising cost of housing, limited housing and the growing lack of diversity in housing options. And then there's the long-term impacts of low wage employment—most often done by women.

50 percent of homeless women on the Peninsula live on less than $500 per month, and at least 23 percent of them have no income at all.

Most homeless women in "paradise" were born and raised in Monterey, had been employed and called the Peninsula their home. They are not here for the iconic scenery of the Central Coast. The dearth of housing development and the loss of employment opportunities grew in the very place they were citizens, and in the neighborhoods where they had invested their lives.

More and more women are being forced into home-lessness at an ever-accelerating pace.

There were at least 500 homeless women on the Peninsula, and perhaps many more who still fail to be counted.

I only had a growing awareness about the lack of emergency and transitional housing options, and had to especially learn about the lack of options for women invisible to the Department of Housing and Urban Development (HUD)—women who are single and with-out children, women who don't have mental illnesses, who are undocumented, disabled, retired or can't work, women who have pets and aren't in recovery from sub-stance abuse. For these women there are very few, if any, options for shelter, safety or community.

Systems that criminalize people who are forced to live outside are built deeply into our municipal codes and cul-tural practices. I had no idea how difficult it would be to try to convince city council members to change ordinances that forbade women to sleep safely in their vehicle, even in the driveway of a friend or member of their own family.

At least 60 percent of women living without ade-quate shelter live in their cars. 70 percent are unaccompanied and live in constant danger.

And there are ordinances and zoning restrictions that disallow the conversion of unused hotel property into residential units. I didn't realize how difficult it would be to convince community members to allow supervised warming shelters in their neighborhoods, even though homeless neighbors were perishing from hypothermia during the cold winter months.

And if you wound up in the emergency room, came out of surgery or were receiving treatment for a serious illness—like chemotherapy for cancer, and you didn't have a place to live, you were back out on the street to convalesce as best you could.

In an ongoing public battle, a neighborhood association in Pacific Grove attempted to prevent the Pebble Beach Company from building affordable workforce housing in the adjacent forest. *The neighbors claimed that a new building would put the trees at risk.*

The company wanted to provide affordable housing for its employees—women and men who were driving miles from near and not so near cities for work. The County Board of Supervisors ultimately stepped in to allow the project to proceed. However, the neighborhood association refused to give up the fight, and asked for revised plans. They demanded the development be turned 180 degrees so that the units would face away from their neighborhood. This struggle has yet to be reconciled and will no doubt continue for many months or even years to come.

And the expenses of creating and sustaining options for the homeless are astronomical.

It costs approximately $400,000 to build a single unit of housing for one person—and that's just *to build it. It costs $20,000 a year to house one woman in a studio unit.*

The Monterey Peninsula boasts some of the most expensive real estate in the country. This means that a significant number of its residents use large portions of their income to meet the basic need for shelter, leaving little for health care, food and other necessities. Consequently, many survive through a delicate balance.

And then there's the competition from vacation rentals, student and workforce housing, and the resultant skyrocketing prices for space that might be affordable.

Only approximately 10 percent of the houses in Carmel are owner occupied; approximately 40 percent in Pacific Grove.

This is not only a local issue; it is a national crisis. It's unusual to pick up any newspaper and not find at least one article on homelessness from a city somewhere in the country.

But I didn't know any of this at first. And soon it was too late. I was quickly too far gone, and still believed naïvely that I could actually make a difference. But looking into the deaths of these nameless, discarded women became the latest iteration of my life's purpose. ▣

FIVE

✛ ✛ ✛ ✛

PREPARATION FOR SERVICE

I N A LONG LIFE, there are many people and circumstances that contribute to who you ultimately become. For me, it was cancer that played a significant role in my evolution. After graduating from seminary in 2007, I was diagnosed with prostate cancer. I decided to have a radical prostatectomy in January 2008, got married later that year and then was ordained an Episcopal Priest in July 2009. My identity continued to morph and whirl out from under me.

Who was I anyway?

That question continued to plague my waking and sleeping hours. I was nothing like who I thought I was, and had no idea what I was becoming. My life seemed to be a never-ending cycle of change, and I needed a way to make sense of it. Loss and grief became my constant companions on a journey that failed to provide a road map, a flashlight or even a flicker of light.

As I write this almost ten years after the fact; it's difficult for me to remember the details but somehow during my recovery, I learned about the Cancer Wellness program at the Community Hospital of the Monterey Peninsula and was encouraged to attend.

A group of cancer patients gathered with friends and spouses on a weekly basis to share feelings, experiences and lessons learned from having cancer. It was facilitated by a well-regarded social worker on the Monterey Peninsula, and it offered me the opportunity for insight, reflection and community.

It was wonderful to have a place to openly share fears and frustrations related to my new identity—"Cancer Patient." Medical professionals had been keenly attentive to ridding my body of cancer, but none seemed available or even interested in discussing what life on the other side of surgery might look like. Being in a safe place with other patients, and shepherded with grace and professional acumen was a gift I will always be grateful for. I made many new friends. Sadly, most would succumb and die over the next several years.

It was in one of those (often tearful) sessions, where Sandy, our facilitator, spoke about the benefits of art. She told us that creativity could provide form and a vehicle to express the effects cancer had in our lives. She talked about writing, dance, exercise, fine art, music and of other modalities for discovering our authentic voice and sharing it in new and surprising ways. Since I am a former dancer and professional movement therapist, this didn't fall on deaf ears. I fully understood what she was encouraging each of us to do, and I began to look for the outlet that was right for me.

One afternoon I went to the campus of Cal State University Monterey Bay (CSUMB) to explore employment opportunities with one of the deans and found an attractive catalogue advertising their Bernard Osher Lifelong Learning Institute (OLLI) for adult learners. The list of class offerings intrigued me, as did the reasonable prices and the absence of grades. These were classes offered for the experience and simple pleasure of learning. The writing courses stood out to me. I had always enjoyed writing, and decided to enroll in a writing circle of about twelve writers, facilitated by the author and scientist Dr. Elin Kelsey. It turned out to be another life-changing experience. Transformation yet again.

I had been made ripe for the plucking, open and full of material to work with. Defenses down, recently out of seminary and just off the operating table, I quickly delved into my life's narrative and explored the landscape I had traveled for almost sixty years. My artifices became transparent, and I felt free to chart the course that led me to this new place of self-discovery. Surprisingly the members of my circle seemed to like my musings and, with constructive criticism, encouraged me.

An essay describing my post-surgery reflections was soon published in a medical magazine. Another essay about aging was then published in a literary journal. Soon I had so much material that I ultimately self-published three collections of personal essays on Amazon. I suddenly became a more thoughtful observer of myself and the world around me, as I continued to document my journey.

While grounded in my tradition of faith, writing encouraged me to be mindful, to engage more fully, to be present and to question what was not immediately understood. It helped me abandon fear and supported the courage needed to enter unfamiliar places. With new awareness, I grew better able to live in ambiguity, with patience and alertness for the answers yet to be formed.

The writing process gave me deeper and broader perspective and helped me realize that I had the resilience and depth to not only persevere, but to thrive; with the hope that there was so much more that lay ahead, on the other side of the unknown.

In the meanwhile, I was invited to serve and continue my work as an ordained priest at St. Mary's. The parish sits in the small sea side community of Pacific Grove. It is quiet, picturesque and uniquely situated on the Monterey Peninsula adjacent to Pebble Beach and its famous 17 Mile Drive. Although a very popular destination for tourists and perhaps because of the very high cost of living, the church had a long history of providing emergency support to people in need.

A ministry called Christian Social Concerns was started decades ago by women who recognized the need to help community members when they fell on hard times. There was a food pantry and thrift shop, and money endowed to provide small grants for utility bills or other outstanding necessities unmet in times of crisis.

My office happened to be outside of where the clients, as we called them, would wait to be seen. As the Associate Rector, I was directly engaged in this ministry and with the volunteers who facilitated it. I did my best to assist in the distribution of resources, enhanced our relationships with other churches and community resources, increased our visibility and supported the education and training of those involved. I had been a nonprofit leader for decades. I knew how to do this. But despite the level of my involvement and my proximity to the people who came to us for help, I had no idea about the extent to which the needs of women living without adequate shelter went unmet. It was in October of 2011 when I received the letter that gave me new eyes, and changed the trajectory of my life. One courageous person met me at my tipping point. I am so grateful that I didn't turn away. ▣

✢ ✢ ✢ ✢

SIX

SECRETS OF THE DEAD

A LARGE MANILA ENVELOPE was delivered to my mailbox at home from the Monterey County Sheriff's office. I was surprised. I doubted. It only took a few days after sending in my check and making a formal request of documents related to the homeless women found dead in Monterey County for it to get here.

There is no anonymity for the deceased. Privacy is relinquished, details reduced to paper and ink, especially for the poor and powerless. The envelope was a tangible reminder that after working on homelessness for five years, there were women still in need of shelter. Women still living and dying outside. The physical evidence of this tragedy now lay bundled in my hands. It was weird. I held the envelope as if I were holding the remains of a loved one, and I was suddenly aware of a deep sadness juxtaposed by a surprising sense of impropriety and intrusion.

Although these were public records, a part of me felt as if I were violating their privacy, looking too close, venturing into some forbidden territory. There was something rather disturbing about the prospects of what I might find. *What I might see.* After all, what on earth was I thinking? I seriously wondered what I actually hoped to accomplish. How far would I be willing to go with this amateur investigation? It suddenly felt fruitless, macabre and a bit unsavory.

Many years ago, while attempting to work on a cadaver in anatomy class, it became clear to me that a career in medicine was not for me. I can't even watch the evening news most nights without turning my head away from the images of war and violence. I didn't really want to read descriptions of rigor mortis or reports of bodies having suffered long term damage or gruesome abuse. So how would I actually get through this review or even begin to navigate such unfamiliar terrain?

As I carried the envelope inside, I decided that, at the very least, I would skim the documents to see what insights I might quickly glean about the lives of these women, and leave the more intimate details unread.

But each report revealed the outline of a very personal story, a brief final chapter of an unaccompanied life once lived outside. Reading page after page, each woman seemed to come alive, the circumstances of her death becoming more real with every word. ▣

Whitney S., White, 72
Pacific Grove, California

DECEASED

Whitney had been a homeless resident of the City of Pacific Grove for many years. A few weeks before she died she went into Hospice care and passed away at a friend's house in Aptos.

She had a sister in Texas. Her sister did not have the money to pay for final disposition. She indicated that there were no other family.

After determining Whitney was indigent and without capable family, she was cremated and the remains returned to her sister in Texas.

Manner of death: Natural
Cause of death: Ovarian cancer

SEVEN

✢ ✢ ✢ ✢

PEELING THE ONION

HOW WOULD I MOVE FORWARD? Five years ago, when I had first received the letter from Joyce, I didn't quite know how to proceed. All I could do was take it one step at a time. I remember thinking, the least I could do was educate myself, and try to discover the truth. In the process, I discovered information that created a pathway—each piece became a stepping stone that took me further into the complicated reality that housing insecurity in "paradise" was indeed a fact that affected many, and was growing worse by the day.

In Pacific Grove alone, the number of homeless women who came to St. Mary's for food, clothing and other resources had increased significantly in the year I received Joyce's letter. When I look at statistics from the first ten months of 2011, I noted that out of 330 persons who were single and homeless, 20 percent were women. I looked further, and through conversations with other clergy and homeless service providers, I learned that the growing number of women who were homeless had outpaced already scarce community resources.

According to available data, there were over 2,500 homeless individuals in Monterey County, and approximately 39 percent were women (which represented an increase of 24 percent from the previous census). And not all were counted. Many were ashamed or afraid to be visible.

The experts all agreed that the most vulnerable and underserved in our communities were homeless women, particularly older women, and those without dependent children, mental illness, domestic violence or substance abuse. This is an important fact worth repeating. I learned that for women like these, the possibility of a bed for the night was becoming more impossible to find. And if you were a woman veteran, you were four times more likely to become homeless than your male counterpart.

Everything I learned about this situation further shocked and haunted me. But I was certain that others would be as well, once they became aware of the need and then given the opportunity to connect with lives and stories that would challenge preconceptions and shatter existing stereotypes. After all, my preconceptions had been shattered. My stereotypes had now forever been discarded.

But I couldn't do anything alone. I needed help. So, I had a conversation with a fellow writer in my writing circle, Kathy Whilden, and asked if she would be willing to join me on this journey. I'm not sure why I asked Kathy. We weren't personal friends at the time. All I knew of her was from listening to her read the essays she shared with the group about her life, and hearing her thoughtful critique of others in the group. She was a priest in the Buddhist tradition, but a woman of similar age and ethnicity to the women who I saw calling out for help. So, I asked her to join me, and she gave me a resounding "yes."

At the time Kathy didn't know what she was agreeing to. Neither of us did. But she agreed to do the smallest thing that we thought possible to achieve. And the journey began with what we thought was just one small step—to make the issue of homeless women visible in our local community.

But before we could help others see, we had to see clearly for ourselves. The first thing we did was contact Joyce, and arranged to meet and listen to her story. We did and quickly realized how large the problem of perception was, how entrenched our own assumptions are, and how static and predictable our perceptions can be about our selves and one another—all open to transformation when we finally met face-to-face. Joyce was African American, smart, articulate and motivated, a victim of circumstance and terrible bad luck. She was kind and caring, nothing to be afraid of, a hero in the making—like a weed growing out of place in a garden, or a flower whose name we hadn't yet learned. We are all strangers until someone says "hello," and we take the time to open our hearts.

I remember the first day I realized that the nuns who taught at St. Gregory's Roman Catholic School in Brooklyn, were human. I mean, I really didn't realize they were people just like me. I must have been around eight or nine, and still thought they were a different kind of species.

One day the wind must have blown up a skirt and I saw a flash of leg, or one of them might have been scratching her neck, and I saw a tuft of hair. But suddenly, somehow, I could see under the habit and discovered a flesh and blood person under the many layers of cloth. A woman behind the veil. From that startling moment, I embarked on a life-long process of differentiating the external facade from what lay within. Even with this conscious objective, more often than not, I chose not to recognize the difference, or even worse, chose one over the other to form my own comforting conclusion.

It was around that time when I was living with my family on New York Avenue in Crown Heights, Brooklyn, New York when my favorite photograph was taken of us. My youngest brother, Richard, had not yet been born.

There we were, my brother Howard and I, our mother and father, all of us dressed to the nines. The apartment was bright and immaculate. We shone with the promise and possibility that was America—success and all that lay ahead. It was beautiful. We looked beautiful. We could have been on the cover of *Ebony* or *Jet*—the "New American Immigrants" issue.

Many years later, when I told my mother that photograph had been my favorite picture of all, she told me that it was taken on one of the saddest days in her life. She didn't tell me the nature of her sadness. I didn't ask. But she said that she did all she could just to stand there and smile.

We were immigrants and had a lot to prove to ourselves, our neighbors and our community here, in the U.S. and particularly to the ones back home in Jamaica, *and* we were black. My parents quickly saw the importance of facade in America. They recognized it as a matter of life or death, and did their best to make sure we always looked our best, dressed well, spoke and carried ourselves above reproach.

There was no room for error or even just relaxing. Outside, at work and play, we were taught to be aware and vigilant about how we appeared to the world in order to assimilate, for upward mobility and for our basic physical safety from those who wanted to do us harm. We had to work hard and achieve, striving always to be (or at least appear to be) perfect.

Consequently, how people and things looked on the outside, was often mistaken for the truth of what was really happening on the inside. My frequent incorrect assumptions about others or situations continued to surprise me and throw me off course. Being alert to external symbols and signs may have, on the one hand, allowed me to recognize what was unsafe, but on the other hand brought me into contact with people and situations that turned out not to be what they purported.

It took many years and experience to hone my discernment. It continues to challenge me and catch me by surprise.

Besides having spent much more time, energy and money on achievement and personal appearance than was actually necessary; what disturbs me the most about this in retrospect, is knowing that I discounted people and experiences solely on how they looked or how I saw them. People and experiences that I missed entirely, that would have probably been blessings to my journey had I been open to them, had I seen them with different eyes.

How many angels went unrecognized? I grieve at how often I must have failed to discover the beauty in things that didn't meet the rigid physical characteristics of what I assumed to be appropriate or acceptable. My narrow vision may have kept me safe, but it was also far too sheltered and parochial.

My father was perhaps the most vigilant about making sure things looked a certain way. He checked his list of criteria for any new person or experience I wanted to engage in. It was always the superficial benchmarks that seemed to matter most to him—criteria I was also supposed to care about. And so, I spent a lifetime building up and looking for the wrong things with my own prejudiced eyes.

Imagine my shock to discover that the beautiful blonde woman working behind the counter was living in her car with all her possessions. I couldn't believe it when a perfectly average looking, middle-aged white woman told me that she was returning to her tent after receiving chemotherapy infusions for cancer. Another had spent all her resources caring for her sick and dying mother, and was now sleeping on the beach and showering in public facilities.

All white, all attractive and well groomed, all hiding the fact that they were homeless. I couldn't believe my eyes. How could I not have seen? How could I not have known? ▣

Brigida A., White, 55
Marina, California

DECEASED

Medics retrieved Brigida from a vehicle which it appeared she was living in. She experienced respiratory failure and cardiac arrest at Natividad Medical Center. She was eventually stabilized and transferred to the cardiac unit of Salinas Valley Memorial Hospital.

It was discovered that she was suffering from Mitral Valve Regurgitation, her echocardiogram revealed her heart was functioning at under 30 percent.

While in the cath lab, Brigida suffered an Acute Myocardial Infarction. Despite all efforts to save her, she passed at 1238 hours on March 23, 2016.

Family for the deceased was located.

It was determined that Brigida had a verbal disagreement with family the evening prior to her hospitalization. As was customary, she had slept in her vehicle. It was parked in Salinas.

Manner of death: Natural
Cause of death: Acute myocardial infarction

EIGHT

✢ ✢ ✢ ✢

BECOMING VISIBLE

O VER TWELVE MONTHS AFTER first receiving the letter from Joyce, and deciding to embrace this new purpose, Kathy and I recruited partners. With the director of the Carl Cherry Center for the Arts in Carmel, we decided to create a photo exhibit that would (ultimately) include the work of documentary filmmaker, Timothy Barrett; photographers, Lina Vitel, Ken Wanderman and Margo Duvall; writer, Erika Fiske; and editors Roxane Buck-Ezcuerra and Patrice Vecchione. The exhibit was to be called "Becoming Visible: The Face of Homeless Women in Monterey County," to introduce the faces and lives of women who were homeless and now chose to become visible. Our hope was that their personal narratives would make a difference in finding solutions for women like them now, and in generations yet to come.

The show ran for five weeks, successfully challenged assumptions about homelessness, and we believed encouraged community action for change. *"We don't want to be invisible, feared or blamed,"* Heidi said. *"We are not dangerous. We only want to be safe and to be given another chance."*

We did our best to share their stories.

This initial step encouraged visitors to open their hearts and minds to the images they saw, and to the voices they heard. We soon recognized that they became more aware of and sensitive to the needs of these members of our community whom most had failed to see. We were moved to discover the means to engage the public to help meet this growing need, and to ultimately help create sustainable solutions for the countless women who live outside. After all, these women were sisters and mothers, daughters and friends. They had found the courage, the strength and dignity to show us who they were. It was finally our turn to show them who we could learn to be as well.

It wasn't a simple process by any means. Kathy and I had our share of opposition and false starts. After assembling the first string of photographers (unnamed here) to volunteer for the project, we met every week for months. Initially they were enthusiastic and quite visionary as we talked about the exhibit and imagined its impact. When it was time for them to go out and begin to photograph the subjects and build content, they claimed they were unable to find compelling material.

One was expected to be able to make appointments with the women, and have them come to a studio or location for scheduled shoots. Another seemed unable to find subjects. The importance of going to where the women were, building relationships and trust, having flexibility and being spontaneous were lessons that still needed to be learned. Ultimately after several months, our first collaborators had to abandon the project and left me, Kathy and the Cherry Center without content.

Starting over was challenging yet beneficial to the process. We were soon able to locate photographers (named above) who were excited about meeting the unique demands of the project. We had learned a great deal from our failures. Learning from our mistakes has been an ongoing theme throughout this journey. We remained open to surprise; we did not give up; we tried to learn from our mishaps, and persevered. When things didn't work out or seem to be going the way that I wanted, I reflected on the women living without shelter. If they could go through what they were going through, I could pick myself up and try again.

That's why I could go on accepting speaking engagements to talk about our project, not having everything in order. I was a priest and knew about fundraising, marketing and public relations, but not much about anything else we were doing. I would simply think of the women under the freeway, or sleeping on the beach, or being victimized in the park and realized that my vulnerability was nothing in comparison to theirs. Kathy always said that we should attempt to do the smallest thing, and not to set our hopes too high or broad in scope. So in the beginning when I went out to speak to groups, I hoped to open just one set of eyes, to soften just one heart. I did, every time.

Yes, I felt invisible too, but I believed early lessons contributed to my willingness to jump into the fray. I think a lot of it had to do with my immigrant background. So much of my life, and the life of my family, had to do with assisting others and building community. And in my family, it all started with Aunt Merce.

Somewhere around 1935, a doctor and his family traveled from New York to Jamaica, West Indies for an exotic vacation. Once there, they discovered the need for someone to care for their children. I'm not sure exactly how, but they secured the services of my mother's Aunt Marcella (known as Merce) who was a nanny during their stay.

When their vacation ended, and the family returned to America, they realized how attached they all had become to Aunt Merce. They arranged for her to immigrate to the U.S.—where she ultimately came to live and work—and became the first one in my family to find shelter in America. To call it "home."

Some years later after the war, Aunt Merce did the same for my mother, who did the same for her sister, who then (many years later) did the same for my grandmother. Over time hands had reached out for many others, providing shelter and safety, community, hope, and making a lasting difference in the lives of family and friends (mostly women helping women) for generations to come.

Perhaps that's why I was shocked to originally discover that there were so many women who lived alone, without safety or adequate shelter on the Monterey Peninsula each night. But I believe that the people of this community are good, and that together, something could be done.

It takes a collection of like-minded people, a community rallying around a common goal with determination and generosity, to create change. Every day the gallery was packed with visitors. The project was received with awe and deeply moved those who experienced it. It was thrilling to witness the response to the portraits and stories of these courageous women who allowed us to share their testimonies and bring the current crises of their lives out from under the shadows. The Becoming Visible exhibit was a complete success.

After the run, the photographs traveled to other venues throughout the county, and was exhibited broadly. It facilitated conversation, inspired invitations for us to speak at countless meetings and events, and encouraged community members to ask themselves, how they could make a difference in this stark reality in our midst. The people of this community are good.

Many said they wanted to contribute money to help broaden the landscape of services for this population of women. But we were not a program, did not have non-profit status, nor did we intend to establish a board and create a new independent organization. Kathy suggested we might consider asking the Community Foundation for Monterey County to serve as our fiscal agent and to establish a fund for us under their umbrella. I thought it was a brilliant idea, and made an appointment to meet with the Executive Director, Dan Baldwin, and Vice President of Resource Development, Christine Dawson. I was honored that they took the time to see me and listened to my proposal. Yes, I was a member of the community but, at that time, I didn't yet have a significant amount of money to invest. Most individuals for whom funds are opened at the Community Foundation present with significant resources. I think we had about $3,000 from thirty caring donors.

I also had passion, vision and the belief that other members of our community would join us and want to donate their resources to help keep women safe. To my surprise, Community Foundation board and staff said "yes" and agreed to my request. Before long, one of their donor advisors contributed $50,000 to establish the Fund for Homeless Women. We had a launch! ▣

Charlene L., White, 58
Seaside, California

D E C E A S E D

Charlene was found drowned in Laguna Grande Lake.

Manner of death: Undetermined
Cause of death: Asphyxia

Barbara R., Hispanic, 41
Seaside, California

D E C E A S E D

Barbara was found drowned in a motel bathtub.

Manner of death: Accident
Cause of death: Asphyxia

Eleanor O., White, 98
Monterey, California

D E C E A S E D

Manner of death: Natural
Cause of death: Failure to thrive

NINE

+ + + +

FILLING THE GAPS

T HE FUND FOR HOMELESS WOMEN was established in 2012 as a field of interest fund of the Community Foundation for Monterey County created to support programs and services for women who are homeless in Monterey County. We decided that although the ultimate goal would be to impact services throughout the county, we would begin with serving women on the peninsula—where we believed the fewer number of services existed, and where we assumed the need was greatest.

We did our best to determine the scope of needs. In my initial quest for information, I made appointments with everyone I could think of who had anything to do with the homeless—beginning with the then Executive Director of the Coalition of Homeless Services Providers, Glorietta Rowland, and through the front-line of service providers themselves.

I was just a parish priest, naïvely entering a territory where they had boots on the ground, every day, some for years. Yet they all agreed to see me. I asked questions, listened intently, probing but never accusatory (I hope). I cobbled together statistics that revealed what seemed obvious to me, and to others who encountered these vulnerable and often desperate women. With existing service programs full, there was just about nowhere to send unaccompanied homeless women for help.

There was a mandated HUD directed census from which we were able to ascertain general numbers, but surprisingly, there was no specific focus given to women. All we could articulate and be driven by was anecdotal information from professionals and the personal stories shared by the women themselves. We hoped to one day go beyond the anecdotal and gather a handle on data that would help us raise money and affect policy decisions. But for the interim, we did what we could, building our case with the evidence we could find.

When I was working at St. Mary's, it was easy for Kathy and me to meet in my office. We met every Wednesday. It was a great way for us to keep the conversation going while getting to know each other. As we met, we allowed the process to unfold and we discovered a path forward. We also invited others to join us in conversation. Doing so helped to expand our understanding of the issues and to develop a circle of support among important stakeholders in the community.

My office at St. Mary's became the de-facto headquarters of the Fund for Homeless Women. And the Parish Hall became the home base for monthly community meetings (which continues to this day). To provide a forum for networking and education, we invited experts in the field to help us build a community of informed members, and to help galvanize a coordinated response to an issue that affects us all.

After a while, it became clear that I needed to decide about how the bulk of my time should be spent. The Fund was demanding more and more of my attention and energy, and I was finding it difficult to do both my job as a parish priest (serving the members of a parish congregation) and as co-organizer of the Fund (which was continuing to grow in scope). Ultimately, I felt that I was being called out of the parish into this unexpected ministry for homeless women.

Doing so meant that I no longer had access to an office, but I requested that we maintain a relationship with the church and continue to use the Parish Hall for monthly community forums.

We became venture capitalists. We knew that there were women out there who needed emergency help for immediate harm reduction, but we also knew that there long-term needs that required sustainable programming that could help women in the future. This bifocal view was how we framed our fundraising. Some got it, many didn't. Most wanted a project that they could go to and perhaps volunteer, a building that they could see and point to, perhaps have their name on the wall. We were a fund providing information and instigating innovation.

Although donors all want to invest in missions toward a greater good, the majority aren't moved to give to a fund, much less to an endowment. Most want to give to a program. And, along with community education and mobilization, we were a fund. We couldn't say it enough, nor did we have any plans to transform ourselves into a service program in the future.

What we hoped to do however, was to incentivize service providers, leverage resources from community donors, and provide venture capital to create innovative programs through our grantmaking that would fill gaps and meet the needs of women who were homeless and not currently receiving services. New programs would be sustained through the point of self-sufficiency, and our endowment would help assure ongoing support for generations to come.

There were programs, good programs, long-standing programs serving homeless people in our area, but women who were single, without dependent children, without a substance dependency or in immediate harm from spousal abuse or a diagnosed serious mental health condition—women who were simply unable to pay market rate rents, had next to nowhere to go for shelter.

This was particularly true for older women (fifty-years of age and older) for whom the future looked dire because of retirement, fixed incomes and their inability to find new or higher paying employment.

We talked to women who had worked their whole lives, but then lost a job, quickly exhausted their savings in rent and found themselves evicted. Women who had been living in situations that quickly changed when owners wanted their property back or increased the rent exponentially. There were former homemakers whose husbands died and were left without a will. Women who were strapped with medical expenses, those who spent all they had caring for elderly parents. Scenario after scenario of women who had lived on the Monterey Peninsula sometimes for a lifetime, who, because of a chain of events (most often beyond their control) were now fighting for their lives without a place to call their own.

So, there were large gaps, and these became our mission to fill. While collecting donations from the community, we concurrently had ongoing conversations with service providers and the women needing to be served. We were on a quest to determine what the best use of our collective resources could be—new, innovative programs that would meet immediate needs, and yet be sustainable in the future, long after we were out of the picture. ▣

Susan B., White, 62
Carmel, California

DECEASED

Susan was found deceased in a transient encampment located on 9th Street at San Carlos Avenue in Carmel. There were no signs of trauma or suspicious activity at the scene.

After an extensive search, it was determined that Susan did not have any next-of-kin. The remains of this transient found in a vacant lot were cremated and scattered on a future date at the Monterey County Cemetery.

Manner of death: Natural
Cause of death: Colon cancer

TEN

✢ ✢ ✢ ✢

THE THREE AMIGOS

WE HAD ADDED a third organizer—Marian Penn, a personal friend of mine who had many years of experience as an accomplished lawyer, nonprofit expert and entrepreneur. I initially contacted her for advice about legal issues related to intellectual property and the photographs in our Becoming Visible exhibit. She was immediately intrigued by what Kathy and I were doing and after attending the exhibit, asked if she could join our effort. We jumped at her generous and enthusiastic offer, and we soon became known at the Community Foundation as "The Three Amigos."

Our friendship and mutual affection for each other has helped sustain us in this work. We each brought a different perspective to every discussion. Our personal, professional and religious backgrounds (Episcopal, Buddhist, Jewish), though different, are complimentary. And we love to make each other laugh. We laugh our heads off during our weekly Wednesday meetings. Unless we are all sick or concurrently out of town we meet every Wednesday and have done so for over five years.

After retiring from St. Mary's and giving up my office in Pacific Grove, we met in various venues around town, inviting others to join us for coffee and conversation. Thank God, we live on the Central Coast of California. We could do that here. And our retreats! We have them in the lobby of Highlands Inn overlooking the Pacific Ocean, followed by lunch at California Market—our special treat, paid for by ourselves.

One-hundred percent of donor contributions go into the Fund. Until getting a grant for administrative expenses from an outside foundation, we used our personal resources to pay for all materials and supplies, printing and mailing.

Our chemistry has worked exceptionally well. There is always someone who is willing to do what the others are unable or unwilling to do. I enjoy public speaking. I also enjoy PR and marketing, so writing letters and designing promotional and fundraising materials is pretty much up to me. Kathy attends community meetings, representing us and gathers information (sometimes covertly) with an unassuming smile. She also has lots of ideas, some I'm sure concocted just to shock us.

Marian thinks that her main purpose in the trio is to provide us with psychological support. We all had to laugh at that one, although, she may have a good point; she is a born strategist. Her mastery of language helps to soften my sometimes hard edges. We also benefit from her optimism, and she knows a lot more people in the community than I do—a major asset when you're fundraising.

I believe one of the keys for a successful partnership is knowing what you are not good at, where you are lacking, and finding other people who can fill the spaces. Diversity is essential. Each of us brings something very different, a unique perspective or reaction, and we make room at the table for all of it, along with the element of surprise. I am usually the most reactive, emotional and eager to take risks. Marian tends to be more thoughtful and strategic. Kathy, brilliant in visioning and the most imaginative, brings us all together to a different reality than the one we believed we were bound to. Most of all, she makes us laugh and reminds us that the challenges we think we need to overcome are not as impossible as we might make them.

I might be shouting at the top of my lungs, with Marian poised in deep contemplation, when Kathy might raise her arms and say, "Wait a minute. Perhaps we should try to expand our imagination. We're not thinking broadly enough." And we are suddenly brought down to a silent pause and a place of new beginnings. Most relevant is our mutual ability to be in a place of ambiguity and unknowing. None of us feel as if any one, alone, has the absolute right answer, or even if there is one. Not knowing is often the acknowledgment that renders courage to wonder, imagine and finally create.

With the help of my friends and now over 1,000 generous members of our community, in the first five years of our working together, we have raised over one million dollars to establish and support programs and services for women living without adequate shelter on the Monterey Peninsula. And, through our annual grantmaking, we have been able to support the opening and/or ongoing operation of five new programs:

> *One Starfish Safe Parking Program — provides safe parking and case management services for women living in their cars. In collaboration with San Carlos Cathedral, we supported the opening and ongoing operation of Gathering for Women — where women receive resources and referrals to a plethora of services and are fed in body, mind and spirit.*

> *Community Human Services received funds from us to increase their ongoing programs for young women. St. Mary's by the Sea, Unitarian Universalist, and the Community Church of the Monterey Peninsula have all been awarded grants to help them meet the emergency needs of unsheltered women and help to keep them safe.*

Because of the generosity of our donors, over time we tripled the amount of money we were able to award to our grantees. And in addition to ongoing support of programs we helped to initiate, we were thrilled to be able to support the creation of twelve units of transitional housing (Women in Transition) and a day program through Community Homeless Solutions. We granted seed money for IHELP for Women and supported temporary housing for homeless women who have mental Illness through Interim, Inc.

Most recently, the Fund for Homeless Women partnered with Housing Resource Center to create a program called SOS—Saving our Senior Women—finding and securing permanent housing for senior women through a comprehensive approach of case management and the education and cultivation of landlords who care in our community.

Together through the work of our partner programs, we have permanently housed over one-hundred women, facilitated emergency safe sleeping for approximately fifty women each night, found employment and/or increased incomes of over seventy-five women, and enabled a combined community volunteer force of over 500 people, mostly women.

This would not have been possible without the generosity of community members who want to make a difference in the lives of women who are homeless, and the partnership of Community Foundation staff who had the vision and the courage to say "yes" when I came to them with outrage and a dream.

In addition to annual grantmaking, the Fund for Homeless Women continues to build an endowment that will support in perpetuity, programs for women living without adequate shelter in our community. And fulfilling our greatest hope, donors have begun leaving lasting legacies by making planned gifts and naming the Fund for Homeless Women in their wills and estate plans. With the Community Foundation, our donors and partner organizations; the Fund for Homeless Women will continue to endeavor to meet the needs of women who are homeless in Monterey County now, and for generations to come.

There is indeed a long journey ahead, before all women who are living without adequate shelter in Monterey County have a place to call home, or at the very least a way to come inside and out of danger. But, this is a beginning—a step like all firsts that needed to be taken. Women were still dying outside. ▣

Paula R., White 38, Monterey
California

DECEASED

Paula was found deceased in a tent at a homeless campsite along a hillside near the intersection of Soledad and Viejo Street, Monterey. She was found by friends. She was unresponsive. Her death appeared natural.

The deceased was homeless and had no family.

While searching the tent, a California ID card was located listing a well-known restaurant on Fisherman's Wharf. Also found was a release form from the Community Hospital of the Monterey Peninsula dated two weeks earlier. The detective recalled having prior contacts with the restaurant owner and knew that he had several employees who had listed his restaurant as their address. The detective called and spoke to the restaurateur and asked him if he knew the deceased. The owner told him that she was indeed an employee of his restaurant.

Manner of death: Natural
Cause of death: Pulmonary thromboembolism

ELEVEN

✝ ✝ ✝ ✝

EMPTY NESTERS

A S THE MONTHS AND YEARS went by, an increasing number of people would come to know and care about the plight of homeless women. The Monterey County Grand Jury ultimately came out with a report about this growing crisis. It was a surprise to us that they were looking into it. We had commissioned a first ever report on the status of homeless women on the Monterey Peninsula, and had no idea that they were as well. Our letters to the editor, showing up at city council meetings, and committing ourselves to educating the community about homeless women seemed to be paying off.

It was reported that the members of the Grand Jury were disturbed by what they were learning about the status of homeless women, and decided to investigate. We reviewed the list of Grand Jury members to see if any were personal connections, but we didn't recognize any of their names. Not one!

The report went into great detail about the lack of affordable housing at the federal poverty level, and described the lack of housing resources particularly for women who lose their income, as well as for those who are older and unaccompanied.

Most surprisingly to many though, was something called the Real Cost Measure statistic which indicated that one out of every three households in California was struggling to meet their basic needs, and that one out of every three persons on the Monterey Peninsula was living at or below the poverty level as calculated by those parameters. According to this measure, one out of every two was economically burdened by housing costs greater than the capacity of their income.

The Grand Jury Report was definitive, authoritative, affirmed our observations and suggested that a lack of leadership and political will was contributing to this dearth of affordable housing, putting the lives and safety of women at great risk.

Consequently, the City Planning Department was buoyed in suggesting the City consider the following recommendations:

1. Legalizing existing 2nd units;

2. Allowing junior units in homes;

3. Repurposing hotels that are no longer filling their intended use;

4. Exploring appropriate policies on short term rentals in the City of Monterey; and

5. Decoupling parking from affordable units.

And although a growing number of community members in the tonier neighborhoods around the peninsula grew more vocal in their opposition, the City Council could no longer defer action. As far as I was concerned, the lack of housing was causing women to die, and that was not acceptable. It appeared others were finally coming to their senses as well.

Yes, we had made a difference. We raised over one million dollars. We had helped to finance the start of five innovative programs on the peninsula, rally and educate a community of citizens about an issue of crisis proportion festering unattended in our midst, and helped to mobilize an army of volunteers. Over 1,500 women were served; one-hundred housed; many employed or otherwise increased their incomes; thirty to fifty were found safe sleeping facilities every night; others were reunited with family members. But there were women still in need of shelter. They were still living (or surviving) and dying outside, and I felt surrounded. It was bad enough to be confronted by the suffering of the living. I was also being haunted by the dead.

In the beginning, we were asked by many individuals to consider forming our own nonprofit organization. Many people offered to be on our board of directors. But we didn't want to become confined to that structure. We felt the need to remain as nimble and autonomous as possible, so that we could react and change as quickly as necessary, having only each other and our supporters to answer to.

Thankfully the Monterey County Civil Grand Jury study of the status of homeless women in the 2015-2016 report loudly affirmed our observations and long-held assumptions. It just so happened that our own assessment of homeless women on the peninsula was completed and published almost at the same time and created a one-two punch in the greater Monterey County community.

Both reports concurred. The needs for women who are homeless, particularly those who are single and older, are many, underserved, vulnerable and growing. Both, but especially the Grand Jury Report, called out for collaborative approaches to long term sustainable solutions but spoke particularly to the need for very low-cost housing and to housing diversity at the very least.

Somewhere in our evolution as a culture of affluence, we discarded the belief that not everyone needed to live in a million-dollar house in a restricted neighborhood overlooking the bay. So, not only did our communities halt development, we eliminated the diversity of housing options, where campgrounds, RV parks and low-income housing, boarding/rooming houses once provided shelter for a range of incomes coexisting as neighbors. Tiny houses could now be added to the list of possibilities.

It was indeed a stunning confluence of events to have both reports completed and made public at about the same time. And the existence of the Grand Jury Report—spurred on by the reportedly persistent articulation of this growing need in our community, spoke highly of the Fund and our persistent efforts to raise public awareness and political will about this crisis. I wrote another letter to the editor; this time in support of the report from the Grand Jury, and was pleased to see it get printed.

I was however very disappointed by what the paper did when reporting this important event. Instead of talking to Kathy, Marian or me, the reporter interviewed representatives from Gathering for Women (a program that we were instrumental in starting and sustaining), and included a photograph of their program in action.

There was no mention of the Fund. Why didn't they ask us for our opinion? Why didn't they make mention of the work the Fund did in contributing to the existence of the investigation, or to the existence of the Gathering for that matter? We were the ones who got the assessment rolling, paid for and sustained it through fruition.

Neither Kathy nor Marian seemed to mind. They never did. Here was a perfect example of how we differed. Maybe it's a male thing. But I have always been more concerned about public relations, marketing and messaging than my amigos. Consequently, I did all the writing to the media, for our fundraising appeals, and outreach materials. I wrote the thank you notes by hand.

I believed it was important that our donors and potential donors heard from us and saw the Fund's name out there in a positive, progressive way, taking a leadership position in the community in addressing these needs.

People want to be a part of something perceived as being out there, boldly doing the right thing. And we were. We are. I didn't want us to be in the shadows. Ever. Not then. Not now. We are advocates of visibility. Never to be found in the dark.

My difference was clear. And I was frequently confronted by that reality. I felt much more protective of our project. While I am perhaps more competitive, exploratory and assertive in forging new partnerships and collaborations, my amigos seemed to be more trusting, conciliatory and patient. It's important for me to know that our work is dynamic, visible, well represented and acknowledged. It's important to them to know that our work is done—even if nobody knows we are behind it.

Being male in this ministry had not been easy and was getting more challenging. Surrounded by women, I was forever mindful of how and when I spoke, and what it was that I chose to say. It hurt when in a group of women, I was overlooked, or my opinion discounted. Despite having dedicated myself to this cause, and serving as a driving force behind these efforts, I was always conscious of the gender dynamic and my position as a gender minority. For a while I couldn't even go to one of our programs. They didn't allow men! And although I understood that intellectually, and respected their policy, I was beginning to feel invisible again in a community that I had given so much of my life and financial resources to support. ▣

Therese L., White, 53
Sand City, California

DECEASED

Therese was found deceased in a pickup parked in the Monterey County Fence Company business yard.

Manner of death: Suicide
Cause of death: Diphenhydramine intoxication

Ariel B., White, 50
Monterey

DECEASED

Sister of the deceased was contacted. Survivors did not have the financial means available to pay for disposition. Ariel's remains were cremated and disposition made in a lawful manner.

Manner of death: Natural
Cause of death: Septic shock

TWELVE

✢ ✢ ✢ ✢

NOW WHAT?

A S WE LOOKED TOWARD 2017 and the Fifth Anniversary of the Fund, it was as if we were stymied. How could we continue to raise money as successfully as we had in the past, when donors seemed to be leaving us to support the very programs we helped to create? How could we raise money for grantmaking while continuing to grow the endowment?

We gave considerable thought to becoming a primarily endowment function. If we felt responsible for providing sustaining funds to programs we helped to establish, would it be responsible for us to continue funding new innovations? And ultimately, when would it be time for us to bow out? And how to do that gracefully?

The Fund arrived at a critical moment in our evolution. We had been instrumental in building a community of informed and responsive individuals who had provided personal resources to meet previously unmet needs. These resources were the venture capital to create viable programs for women to the landscape of services on the Monterey Peninsula. While granting almost one million dollars over three annual cycles, we had a small but growing endowment providing spendable income equal to about 5 percent of its total.

We were in the process of producing two new fundraising events, which would increase and enhance our visibility and donor pool, and were in the beginning stages of brokering a collaboration with the Monterey Museum of Art, California State University Monterey Bay, and our service provider agencies to mount an exhibit of photographs taken by women who are homeless in our communities.

Additionally, because of our comprehensive assessment of the status of homeless women on the Monterey Peninsula, an expanded assessment was planned to include the entire county. These, along with the Grand Jury assessment could provide the data needed to substantiate our efforts and strategically measure our success.

Another accomplishment was our monthly community meetings, to which we invited a guest speaker to present an aspect of homelessness or issue in service delivery. We found that with the complexity and nuances inherent in homelessness, we needed constant education and reality checking, and decided early on to bring our donors and "friends" along with us. This shaping and building of an informed committed community turned out to be incredibly helpful from all perspectives. Not only had we been raising funds and building programs, we had been raising friends. But we weren't sure what should happen next.

However as fledgling programs (initiated and sometimes maintained by Fund support) developed their systems and infrastructure, and grew more self-sufficient, their donors and volunteers became more numerous. We wanted these programs to thrive! The Fund constantly endeavored to neither compete nor even give the appearance of competition for support. (This was particularly the case with Gathering for Women who initiated a capital campaign for the purchase of a permanent location out of which to provide services.)

While the Fund continued to encourage and support the capacity building of these community programs, we began to experience a growing depletion of our own donor pool and financial resources. Some donors became confused by the sudden proliferation of service organizations asking for contributions; others wanted to give directly to the programs in which they could volunteer and observe. Most wanted their gifts to be used directly and expediently, without going to an endowment or through a regranting process. Given this reality and frequent confusion in community brand perception, the need for a reclarification and recalibration of the Fund's identity and current goals were both timely and critical.

Looking toward the future, we knew that the status and needs of women who are homeless on the Monterey Peninsula would change, as would the economy and our various government's support of programs for women who are poor. Serving only women, none of the programs we helped to initiate were eligible for federal funds. That prohibition would probably never change. Though difficult to predict the direction, the existence of employment opportunities and affordable housing inventory in the community would change as well.

Equally relevant would be the inevitable emergencies and changes (staff, financial, etc.), which would be experienced by service organizations themselves, and affect their ability to carry out their work in the community to serve this population.

Existing programs would need ongoing financial assistance to build capacity and support their daily operations. New innovative programs would need venture capital to launch—particularly for the development of housing inventory and related programs for shelter.

It was and remains our vision that the Fund for Homeless Women would remain fiscally viable in both spendable and invested assets sufficient to carry out the next phase of its work—supporting existing and new programs for women who are homeless on the Monterey Peninsula in current and future generations.

Focusing on the "big picture," the Fund also envisioned itself as an ongoing facilitator for community education and mobilization, encouraging awareness building in order to ultimately ameliorate this human tragedy.

We had journeyed to a critical point in the Fund's life cycle and were provided the opportunity to clarify its focus and transition its fundraising strategy from primarily current needs to long-term growth and fiscal sustainability. To help facilitate this vision, the Fund for Homeless Women would need:

- *Rebranding.* A new public relations and marketing strategy was needed to clearly articulate who we are, what we do and where we want to go; delineating our relationship to our program partners, and differentiating us as a fund distinctly different from service programs in the field (which we were instrumental in creating).

- An agreement from its grantees to publicize its relationship to the Fund and being beneficiaries of Fund for Homeless Women grants.

- Transitioning from our primary strategy of raising funds for spendable regranting, to endowment building (or some percentage combination of both).

- Pivoting to an endowment fundraising program with a plan to solicit major planned estate, real estate, stock and cash gifts for long-term sustainability.

- Attaining an endowment worth five million dollars to generate 250 thousand dollars of income for annual grantmaking.

All of it is easier said than done. In our ongoing effort to work collaboratively with diverse partners, and in a climate of transparency we invited a group of our most invested donors to meet for conversation and planning. We discussed our challenges, articulated our benefits, restated our vision and began to chart a way forward. Although we had accomplished a great deal in the first five years, there would be much more to do in the years ahead. ▣

Lisa K., White, 51
Seaside, California

DECEASED

Lisa was found dead in a Hotel Room in Seaside. The detective obtained prescription pill bottles left on the nightstand in the room. Prescriptions were for Hydrocodone and Valium after being treated at the Community Hospital of the Monterey Peninsula.

Also found were keys to a white BMW parked in the lot outside. Further investigation found that the vehicle was registered to her son. He was advised of his mother's passing and information was given to him on what might have occurred. He was asked if he wanted his car towed or if he would pick it up. He said that he would pick it up later that day.

Further conversation was had with a social worker at Community Hospital who advised the officer that she had been working on Lisa's case, and was expecting Lisa to see a psychiatrist in the next few days to deal with what might have been a state of depression.

Manner of death: Suicide
Cause of death: Acute polysubstance intoxication

THIRTEEN

✛ ✛ ✛ ✛

FINDING OUR WAY

O N A TRIP TO SAN FRANCISCO, my spouse Bill and I visited the new Museum of Modern Art. The architecture and contemporary art were compelling and moved me in body, mind and spirit. We started on the main floors housing their permanent collections and then moved up to the photography and sculpture galleries.

All the rooms were interconnected by wooden pathways and beautiful staircases. There are seven floors and the higher we went the more avant-garde, broken, open and deconstructed the work seemed to become. The architecture provided an organic context for the art, framed by shadows and the natural afternoon light.

All the components existed in partnership. The individual elements were juxtaposed in a way that seemed harmonious, while making space for an interactive and emotionally accessible experience.

Cameras were strategically placed throughout the museum, so that images of the visitors themselves could be projected on screens. Patrons became part of living art. All of us—voyeurs—watching and being watched by countless others.

Although I was aware of being impressed by the work, the deeper effect this experience was having on my psyche went unnoticed until (after having gone through almost all the galleries and toward the very end) I walked out on to a balcony on the top floor, and looked out onto the enormous landscape of San Francisco. It appeared the art continued far into the distance.

I stepped out onto a divine canvas. Creation was growing in one place, deconstruction happening in another. People and other animals coexisted among trees, earth and sky. Skyscrapers and elevators, freeways and vehicles were layered and intertwined for as far as my eyes could see.

There were no clear lines of distinction between the sacred and the secular. All were one, and each person, each object was an integral part of a living mosaic. Living that became a sort of worship, and bodies whose mere existence was like prayer.

I had the distinct feeling that after this experience in the museum, I would never view the world in quite the same way again. That it had offered me, yet again, a new way of seeing.

This is exactly what I believe happened with our first exhibit in Carmel. Becoming Visible helped begin to change the perspective of its viewers when seeing and thinking about women who are homeless. People in our community thanked us for not only starting the conversation, but for opening their eyes and hearts to a growing population of neighbors needing the attention and help from people who for the most part were unable or unwilling to see them.

We hoped that a new exhibit, planned for the spring of 2017, called "What We See—Photographs by Women Without Shelter" would do the same thing, but at the next level, with the women now taking pictures of their world, showing us the landscape as they see it, and telling more of their own personal stories.

Taking this approach, we hoped to move the viewer to a deeper perspective and compassion. And perhaps it would be more meaningful for the homeless participants—who themselves would be creating the art and given a platform where it could be experienced and appreciated by others. We felt the time had come.

I often think of the line by the poet, Langston Hughes, who wrote "What happens to a dream deferred?" Social systems have resulted in the intentional disenfranchisement of many groups, here and abroad. After centuries of social injustice, where laws and mores have kept women and minorities in position of social and economic disadvantage, the devolution to housing instability and economic vulnerability for so many was inevitable. It was only a matter of time before the ultimate outcome became visible, our complicity more obvious, and a call to action more distinct.

Initially, most people couldn't understand what we

were doing. It felt like so many people had a suggestion or a solution that they thought we should be working on. Getting people to accept the fact that we were a fund and not a program continued. Instead of harm reduction and emergency services—providing immediate safety, why weren't we building tiny houses, converting motels or building shelters? Why were there no beds? Why didn't service organizations have the capacity to expand programs? Why were there so many organizations and no central intake procedure or one place where women could go to for help?

It took a long time for us to understand the complexity of the problems, and to find the language to articulate answers that no one seemed to want to hear. Although we were gaining traction and increasing our fundraising revenue, donors held on to their expectations, their hopes that we would magically and immediately create shelters—places were these women could go. There were also service providers who feared that our fundraising was going to diminish theirs—like ours impacted by programs we funded. How dare we enter a pond where others had been swimming for years? How dare we assert that they were not meeting all needs, and also solicit funds from a community of donors whom they had already cultivated? For many, we were naïve and brazen competitors.

Early on we even got flak from some homeless women who expected the Fund for Homeless Women to be a fund for homeless women—like a bank for personal resources where one might withdraw cash from an ATM. There are some who still think that, and deride us for not using the funds that we raise in the way that they demand for their own personal and unique needs.

We benefit from having the Community Foundation for Monterey County as a partner in this collaboration. They have been instrumental in shaping policy and protocol for granting, vetting the grantees and assuring proper use of funds disbursed. Most of our donors approve, but there remains some who are disgruntled.

After raising over $30,000 in one fundraiser for the Fund, a group of volunteers then threatened to keep the proceeds. They didn't approve of the policies established by the Community Foundation, and wanted the money to be used immediately and in the way that they saw fit. Some wanted us to establish a board of directors on which they would sit.

Who had given us the authority to do what we were attempting, they asked. Ultimately, they relented, and the money was turned over, as the event donors intended, and many of these "volunteers" moved on.

Certainly, we have had our share of growing pains, but none too severe to impede our momentum, cloud our vision or prevent us from finding our way. And even as we faced turning points in our journey, we moved ahead with optimism.

We were passionate about our mission and shared a deep sense of compassion for the women we hoped to serve. We had a growing understanding of the complexity of the issues, and continued to stay fully engaged with appropriate stakeholders. But perhaps more than that, we weren't afraid to fail or move forward in ambiguity. Although we didn't fully know what lay ahead, we could step out into the unknown with courage and conviction. We attempted to give voice with confidence that the financial investment we gathered would be used thoughtfully, without wasteful overhead, and as intended by the donor entrusting us with their resources. And throughout it all, we were having so much fun. In that context, opposition was a mere inconvenience at its worse, and a teachable moment at best.

Like those who were frustrated with us, we were sometimes frustrated by what appeared to be a lack of capacity on the part of some service providers to expand their services. Most of the service organizations struggled to support their existing programs, and couldn't afford to add additional components to their service delivery systems. Some appeared to be immobilized by the fear of "mission creep." Some struggled with staff and leadership, others with vision, at least that's how it often seemed to us.

Kathy continued to insist (rightly), that we needed to help expand the argument beyond "housing stock" and "affordable housing." The word "affordable" is after all, problematic in and of itself. What most call "affordable," is definitely not so for someone who is homeless.

The contemporary phenomenon of urban gentrification and the "upscaling" of housing in cities and counties around the nation has resulted in the absence of housing options for people at the very bottom—what many call "low-low income." So we have come to a better (or at least our) way to frame the problem by thinking of it as more than the need for affordable (or even low-low income) housing, and to rather think of it as the need for diversified housing; from places to camp to places to park—a variety of housing options that meet a variety of budgets. Our community didn't have that. We all aspired to live like the characters on "Big Little Lies." But how many of us can do that?

For many individuals, support services are essential to maintaining housing and personal well-being. But some form of housing must exist in the first place. And for a growing number of people in Monterey County, that was just not their reality. You don't have to be a poor woman to experience this. From retirees to young professionals, Monterey County residents were being forced into homelessness at an alarming rate. Salinas has the fastest escalating market rate for housing in the county, and possibly the entire state. If you couldn't afford to move to Salinas, where could you go?

To feed our spirits, we decided to convene a writing group for homeless women in the public library (another one of Kathy's ideas). She read about a similar group in another state and thought it might work here with us. I agreed. The head librarian was actively engaged in the homeless issue in Monterey, and attended a meeting Kathy and I went to at Monterey Public. We soon arranged to meet her and her staff there. Everyone concurred and arranged for us to start a writing group in just a few weeks.

I was particularly looking forward to it. I missed the personal contact, and the compelling stories of the women I had dedicated myself to help. It would be for women only—and me. I totally understand the reluctance of some to be in a mixed gender environment, especially when art demands emotional vulnerability and self-exposure. But I no longer had frequent direct interactions with homeless women. This distance was not nurturing for me, as I continued to advocate on their behalf.

And so I hoped that if the women agreed, I would be allowed to participate, and that it would be of benefit to all of us to write and share our stories. But I would have to figure out if, in this context, was I more impediment than facilitator—now too visible and an obstacle?

The group was never as well subscribed as we had hoped. We wondered why, asked the few participants, changed the name from "Facing Hard Times" to "Writing with Friends." Although women said they were interested and planned to come, few did. But those who did seemed to have a meaningful time.

Although we had asked the attendees, I wondered if my presence was the cause for more women not to attend our writing group. The question was posed broadly at the Gathering, and the response was that it wasn't about me at all. In fact, I was known, liked and wanted. Upon hearing the suggestion that I not attend, one woman said, "Now that is the most ridiculous thing I have ever heard." So, I continued to attend. Most importantly, we asked the question, asked them what it was that they wanted, and ensured we were not imposing ourselves and our assumptions on them. ▣

FOURTEEN

✢ ✢ ✢ ✢

NEIGHBORHOODS

THE MONTEREY PENINSULA is not unlike other places I've lived in before. Symbols of class and affinity are significant even in a place many call paradise. Perhaps more than what you wear or drive; where you live can be a primary marker of who you are in the eyes of others, how you feel about yourself and to which tribe you ultimately belong or are assigned to. People who are homeless are no different. They need community as much as anyone else. And they want it to be in the place most have called home long before becoming homeless—a place they were proud of.

I was prepared for this phenomenon before moving to California's Central Coast. While growing up in Brooklyn, there were few things I wanted more than to move out of Flatbush and into Manhattan. Consequently, I lived on the Upper West Side of New York for ten years of my life before moving to Los Angeles—where I lived in Westwood (on the West Side) and Valley Village surrounded by Encino, Toluca Lake and Studio City.

There was very little pride in being considered a "bridge and tunnel" person. It was just one more barrier, one more label projected on to people like me—living on the outside, on the outer edges of the Big Apple. And there were thousands of us migrants who crossed the river daily by any means necessary.

Brooklyn has come a long way since the days of my youth. Gentrification and upward mobility have created a sort of golden borough where mostly artists and seekers, working class people and folks from immigrant backgrounds like my family once got their start. Before "diversity" became a cultural imperative, mixed or transitional neighborhoods were synonymous with poverty and was a reality from which many attempted to escape.

Neighborhoods become context, stages or platforms for the living of our lives and contribute to how we move in the world, experience each other, and express ourselves. They provide us with community and a sense of belonging.

Addresses are not mere numbers and words, places where you just happen to land. For most, they describe social location and class, desire and vision, value and priority. They articulate aspiration and accomplishment.

Our neighborhoods keep some people in and others out. They describe groups and create boundaries—geographic, economic, educational and cultural. Where you live really does matter. And when you finally arrive at where you want to be, you do what you can to protect it. Consider decades of restrictions that created and sustained segregated communities, preventing those deemed unworthy to move in next door.

My parents traveled to America and raised me during a time of national prosperity, prolific capitalism and social striving. Remember TV shows like *The Jeffersons, The Beverly Hillbillies, Green Acres* and even *Mr. Rogers?* They were all about neighborhoods, belonging and moving up.

I was raised on that stuff. They shaped me and fed my dreams of home, security, neighbors and community. I'm certainly not unique in that regard. So who was I to tell anyone to pack up their stuff and move to Bakersfield? It would only be a matter of time before my neighbors in Monterey would rally the troops in preparation for an upcoming City Council meeting, and a much-anticipated discussion about locating an emergency homeless shelter in the neighborhood (furthest away from the Monterey city center and its other more affluent neighbors). Nothing is accidental. City planning and the making of neighborhoods is a strategic, complicated and sometimes covert process. However, block associations and community groups have and continue to play an important role in what happens where, when and why.

The folks in my working-class neighborhood were mad as hell and very much afraid. Grumblings about homeless encampments, burglaries and strangers wandering the streets had been occurring for over a year and continued to increase over time.

The Neighborhood listserv constantly displayed posts written by fearful property owners concerned about their safety or complaining about noise, trash and illegal overnight parking. The homeless had become the target of anger and scapegoating, and the neighbors felt that they had enough.

I was an advocate for the homeless. I wanted shelter and affordable housing. It's ironic that this intense struggle had literally found its way into my own backyard.

Bill and I had long standing plans to be in San Francisco on the day of that much-anticipated council meeting. Apparently, the neighbors were contentious and came out in full force. Unable to complain about trees being at risk (like the folks in Pacific Grove protesting the development of affordable housing near their neighborhood), or (defensively) alleging concern over homeless women being victimized by their male counterparts on Solano Ave (preventing the operation of a warming shelter there); my community noted it's already high density, and presented the argument that a homeless shelter in close-proximity to an elementary charter school would not be a good idea. Don't mess with angry charter school parents. Consequently, a decision was postponed. This time, until after the election of a new City Council.

Another winter was approaching and still, despite a state mandate for every county in California to provide appropriate emergency shelter for its citizens, no legitimate emergency shelter plan had been developed in the city of Monterey. In anticipation of inclement weather, and in light of stringent sit and lie ordinances, the City of Salinas was successful in creating a public-private partnership and announced the opening of a temporary warming shelter during the upcoming winter season. It would be managed by Community Homeless Solutions (CHS)—an organization for whom we had provided seed funding and continued to support.

For three years CHS had offered to run a similar shelter on the peninsula if the city and county collaborated and offered the use of one of their unused or underutilized buildings. But nothing would be found as suitable. No neighborhood would be deemed appropriate. No empty spaces would be made available before the torrential rains returned in another winter.

In fulfillment of the grant applications for 2016, Fund for Homeless Women grantees presented reports of how monies they received from us the previous year were used to provide stable and permanent housing options. Kathy ran the numbers and garnered that through our program partners, Fund for Homeless Women resources helped serve over 1,500 women, assisted the housing of 100, and was providing safe emergency sleeping for approximately thirty to fifty women every night. Together our program partners had mobilized a volunteer force of over 500 committed volunteers.

We also figured out that (according to statistics offered) about thirty new women become counted as homeless on the peninsula each year. How could we engage them on the front end, and stop them from entering that pipeline at all? Certainly there needed to be more options for housing diversity and affordable housing, but we also needed continued investment in prevention.

In the meanwhile, my neighborhood continued to rally the troops to try to prevent it from being zoned appropriate for the homeless. Community meetings were suddenly planned and announced over various listservs. One was organized on behalf of public awareness and engagement to be held in the school auditorium. I was scheduled to speak to the Corral de Tierra Rotary Club at the same time and couldn't attend.

City staff were scheduled to engage and inform my neighbors about the proposal to deem our area as a "zoning overlay" which qualifies it for the development of emergency homeless shelter—which the city of Monterey had been mandated by the state to provide somewhere in the city since 2007. State Senate Bill 2 required jurisdictions to identify areas where emergency shelters for the homeless would be permitted without requiring notification. And because public notification was not required, the sudden announcement of a proposed zoning overlay was being met by my neighbors with surprise, anger and resignation.

In anticipation of this meeting the neighborhood association spread the news about the potential of what they considered "catastrophic." Parents of children at the charter school located well within (if not in the center of) the triangle where the shelter had been proposed, were poised to attend in protest, as were others from the neighborhood.

For days after the meeting I combed the paper and internet looking for information about what had transpired and to learn more about the proposal. Finally, someone who attended the meeting posted a letter on our neighborhood listserv who wrote to City staff in reaction to the meeting. Most informative to me was the following:

> *"...As I have mentioned previously this is an area known by both the Seaside Police Department and Monterey Police Department as having a huge problem with homelessness, vagrancy, drugs, violence and crime. To place a 500 bed shelter next to an area that is known to all law enforcement as a problem area, just doesn't make sense. As a community, we have been active in making this a safe place for everyone.*
>
> *I have spoken with my neighbors and we want to understand your proposal and the reasons for your decisions. But I fear your proposal will make all our previous efforts just a waste of time."*

> *KB.*

A 500 bed shelter! I couldn't believe it. That couldn't possibly be correct. They don't build shelters like that anymore, anywhere. It all sounded so unlikely that I was amazed by what people believed they had heard and talked about. What was also reinforced by this and other comments was the sentiment that a shelter of any size was not wanted here, particularly in close proximity to a charter school, and certainly not in a neighborhood of working class people who didn't want their property values (in what might be the last affordable neighborhood in the city of Monterey) to be diminished. Someone replied:

> "What I have found particularly disturbing is that, had we not caught this, it would have been voted on by the council without our input. That concerns me tremendously. One can only imagine what may have already been put through, and what they plan on trying to do this way in the future. Hopefully, after this incident, City staff will see that they cannot push things over on us who live on this side of town."

> RB.

And that was only the beginning.

> "I really believe that we should push for the entire City to be part of the zoning changes so that the brunt of the State requirement for an area to be identified and rezoned to allow homeless emergency shelters won't fall on our area alone. The City needs a comprehensive plan, not a knee jerk reaction. I think our area was an easy solution since we are the only blue collar/affordable area in Monterey. The City likely thinks we will have less resources to put up a fight."

> JJ.

"Bottom line is that the rezoning proposal offered by the City needs to be opposed. The influx of shopping carts, lines of homeless waiting to get into a shelter each afternoon, and the predictable increase in thefts will have a huge impact on our area. Yes, the homeless need shelters. Many of us are only a few paychecks away from their plight... but these shelters could be spread throughout the city, not congregated in one 15 acre zone."

JJ.

"Years ago, the neighborhood was split in half when they put in the freeway. Now they want to inflict our neighborhood with shelters for the homeless."

KB.

"Luckily we caught it BEFORE the council vote."

EM.

"More residents have to get involved and express their concerns about the homeless population being redirected to where they live, and they need to question everything!"

KS. ▣

FIFTEEN

✛ ✛ ✛ ✛

A NATURAL WOMAN

WHEN OUR HOUSE was being painted, I went to the paint store to select white paint and discovered more shades of white than I had ever imagined. After spending hours collecting samples and placing them all around the house to make what we thought was the best selection, we were amazed at how different the colors looked in different rooms in different light. Each was unique depending on what was in the room, on the floor, and whether we had our glasses on.

That experience became a perfect metaphor for this project. Every step we took changed our perspective. Everything learned sharpened our focus, and helped us see just a little bit more clearly what we were dealing with and all that needed to be done. The evidence was everywhere. We couldn't see where we were ultimately going, but that's another story. I was often asked, "So what is the big picture? What do you ultimately want to accomplish?" Besides stable housing for women who needed it, services that filled in the gaps, increased public awareness and community engagement, I couldn't be more specific.

Many things continued to contribute to shaping my perspective on the issue of homelessness and our work within it. My attendance at the USC Department of Social Work and the American Roundtable to Abolish Homelessness conference is a good example. Besides affirmation, the entire experience provided a broader context and more information than I had ever been exposed to. The presenters offered scientific research, data, reports of studies, regional and national portraits of the status of unaccompanied women, causes and solutions for homelessness. It resulted in both broadening and clarifying my very naïve and parochial perspective.

I discovered that most women who are homeless in urban settings were older and victims of trauma. I was also interested in finding out that, although rehoused, without ongoing support by case management staff, most of these women continued to be victimized, and often found themselves unable to maintain themselves in permanent shelter.

It was pointed out that women and men are indeed different. Causes and solutions for homelessness are therefore different for women, as is the way services are provided and individuals approached. What women value (community, reciprocity, an opportunity to self-actualize and offer her gifts to the world), are not necessarily the primary values of men. Success and safety are not seen in exactly the same way.

Trauma seemed to be the overriding theme that ran through the cases presented at the conference. Without first dealing with trauma, services were for the most part, inaccessible. As it was explained, if a woman did not become homeless because of trauma, the experience of homelessness was in itself traumatic and left a more significant and lasting effect on a woman than it appeared to in their male counterpart.

Looking back, I finally understood the desperation and laser-focused intensity experienced in my prior interactions with women who were homeless. Traumatized, vulnerable, unprotected and uncertain of her future, these women could only be concerned about their sustenance, safety and protection. For that moment in their lives, nothing else mattered.

It was our hope that the What We See exhibit at the Monterey Museum of Art, which marked our fifth anniversary, would help season and further clarify the perspective of the attendees. A similar exhibit created by homeless individuals in Paris was successful in meeting those objectives. When I was in France in 2016, I visited the organizers and discussed their processes and challenges. Our conversation was very enlightening, and provided me with an international perspective, and contributed to the evolution of how I saw the issue. It's all about perspective. And while allowing ourselves to be changed, we were attempting to help shape the way others saw it as well.

While planning the exhibit, Marian, Deborah (guest curator for the MMA exhibit) and I drove to the Stanford

University Virtual Reality Lab. We went to experience their virtual reality protocol for homelessness and we quickly found ourselves in a brand-new world.

Standing in the middle of a large room, I was attached to an apparatus suspended from the ceiling, my eyes were covered by oversized goggles. I didn't have an opportunity to choose my virtual experience, but was given one called "The Plank." Suddenly the floor seemed to open beneath me to reveal a large dark hole, over which lay a plank. Although gently guided by the lab staff, I was terrified. My panic must have been noticeable because I heard Marian say, "Don't worry Michael, you won't fall in." The sound of her voice and her words were reassuring, but it didn't stop me from having a dramatic physiological reaction. I began to hyperventilate and sweat.

The lab staff gently suggested that I walk on the plank. Again, my hesitancy, body language and deep breathing must have alerted her because she said, "You don't have to do anything you don't feel comfortable doing." After which I quickly removed the goggles and leaned against the wall. For some reason, the experience was so vivid that my brain couldn't fully differentiate between the real and the virtual. I was in danger, and felt as if I was going to fall into a deep dark hole.

Later three young visitors from Google came in for a demonstration. We stood back to observe them. After going through a few experiences of their choice, I suggested that they try "The Plank." They did, but seemed to enjoy it. For them it was an adventure. I assumed they had more experience with video games than I did. My brain hadn't been exposed and formed in that way. I couldn't tell the difference between real and virtual. All I saw and felt was trauma.

The homeless experience was equally compelling. It came in three scenarios of about five minutes each. In it you were the subject and the voice was female. The first encounter occurred in an apartment where the landlord was banging on the door demanding you pay the rent or face eviction. You then had to decide which objects were left in your apartment to sell, so that you could make your rent payment. Gradually everything in the room was sold, but it did not produce enough cash to cover your debt, and you were evicted.

The next scenario had you living in a car, surrounded by clothes and the belongings you had left. While parked for the night and trying to find a toothbrush, a police officer suddenly shines his light in the window, and in a harsh tone of voice demands that you move on.

In the final scenario, you are riding a three-hour bus route in the middle of the night—the only option you have for sheltered sleep. While sitting there, you are a potential victim and need to keep alert and aware of men approaching you to harm you or steal your belongings.

I was totally drawn in. Clearly this was not real. I was not homeless. But I felt empathy. I was deeply moved and could barely speak when the demonstration was over. I knew women who lived this experience every day. To me it was very real, and a useful tool to raise awareness of the reality of homelessness. Moving it from an intellectual construct to an experienced human condition.

It just so happened that one of the young Google guys who danced over the plank earlier was watching while Deborah went through the homeless demonstration. As soon as it was over (having not gone through the experience himself) he began a barrage of questions. "Well, what's the purpose of that?" "What can you do with that? I mean, I guess it's well done but how can that actually help change the homeless situation?" We were clearly from two different worlds. I was convinced that building empathy was the ultimate key, or at least was a potentially effective step toward active engagement and creating change.

More accessible than virtual reality and perhaps even more successful in building empathy is hearing the compelling stories of the women who live in and survive these challenging circumstances. Describing who they are, participants in the What We See exhibit told us just that. The following personal statements were offered with permission by the participants in the exhibit called, What We See: Photographs by Women Without Shelter, Monterey Museum of Art:

Anonymous

Who am I?

I'm originally from the Bay area in CA. I came from a very wealthy but greedy family. I have a master's degree in international Policy Studies. I have had great jobs. I was once an athlete, a runner, and I volunteered extensively in my community. I did and still have a great singing voice. I sing in church. I was just one of those high Type-A personalities who did it all. Life was good. Then health circumstances just kept happening to me and I became homeless.

I do tell people about my disabilities, but I don't tell people that I'm homeless. I remain anonymous so I don't get stigmatized. The systems to help people out are not the best and you can find yourself on this spinning wheel: go there, do that, try this, try that, when talking to people about needing services. I'm grateful for my friends who help me. I am staying in a motel for now. Thank God, because it's so cold outside. ∎

Debra

Who am I?

I was born in Seaside, CA. My mother moved there from the south because she had family there. I grew up in the old Seaside neighborhood, playing up top of Broadway, when at the time there were no homes, just sand and bushes, and a great view. Every time I ever thought of moving on or leaving this area, I'd just turn around, look at the ocean view, and think there is no better place. It's beautiful here. It's my home.

When I first heard the announcement of this photography exhibit, I thought now what kind of pictures could I ever take to be part of a museum show. So, I decided to do a collaboration and take pictures with my young granddaughter. What a privilege it was to have this opportunity to work with my granddaughter and have this great memory for us both. Something I would not have been able to do on my own. You see, I don't have a lot of friends. I'm alone a lot, so this was a great moment in time for me because it felt like something normal in my life. ∎

Kelly

Who am I?

I'm originally from West Virginia. I went to really good Christian schools. My mom worked hard for her kids to go to these good schools. I ended up at George Washington University. I left GWU and got a job with AmeriCorps in a program called For the Love of Children. It was a good job, and I loved it. I taught 6th through 8th grade kids to read and write. AmeriCorps made me interested in what people were doing, especially those struggling on the streets. To me, this had value.

Growing up in West Virginia, I didn't learn how to make money or how to take care of myself. So, I came to California to see my mom. I didn't have money, clothes, or food, and so I got sick. The doctor gave me meds. After that, my mom didn't want me around. She couldn't take care of me. So, I gravitated towards the streets and bars where I was raped and traumatized. I am healing now. I am trying to let go of much resentment. As odd as this may sound, I would like to help kids; kids that are dealing with violence in school. ∎

Liz

Who am I?

I'm originally from Los Angeles. I had been dealing with homelessness for about three years traveling up and down the state when I stopped in Monterey. I had a friend named Rana who told me about getting help at the Gathering for Women. I'm now living with my parents in LA. I will be having a baby boy soon. My dreams for baby and I are to be stable and to make a good living. I just want him to grow up happy and healthy. I've been interested in the arts as work. But I'm exploring other avenues as well. ∎

Marie

Who am I?

I lost my job at an upscale bed and breakfast in Carmel due to an autoimmune problem that affects my skin. The owner saw me when I was having a flare up on my face. A week later I was fired. For now, I am renting out a garage illegally with no plumbing, electricity or water. But this location keeps me in my old neighborhood of Old Monterey. I like Monterey. It's my home. ■

Patty

Who am I?

I was born in Salinas. I have six children and a bunch of grandkids. I came to Monterey to go to Monterey Peninsula college. Yep, back to school at fifty-three. I took classes in art and ceramics. I even took classes to learn about grant writing. Soon after, I got a job with a program where I helped recovering women live a sober life. It felt good to give back and to help where I could. It was an amazing job. I have seen too many women not believe in themselves. This is why they don't help themselves and end up homeless. I help at the women's homeless shelter. I drive the van that picks them up to take them to get human services. It feels good to help when and where I can. ■

Regina

Who am I?

I am 46, single, and well looking. My best friend's name is Tweety, and she goes everywhere I do, as she is also a service dog. I was born in Southern California, living in cities such as Malibu and West Hollywood. I went to Pasadena Community College and excelled in photography and journalism. I did an internship at the LA Times working as a photographer/editor. I used to have an office and studio in West Hollywood. I was raised in a Real Estate family. Hence I have a real estate license and property management background as well.

I came to Monterey for a job interview, but the job didn't go through. So, I was out of work for a while with nowhere to live. Eventually, I found Gathering for Women and they helped me get a job at a local hotel resort in marina. They provided me with clothes for a job interview. They gave me a voucher to shower at Veterans Park, which is very cold by the way. Most important they gave me a gas card to get around.

When you are homeless, having the means to get gas, clothes, a shower, and a laundry card makes all the difference in the world. Gathering for Women volunteers go out of their way every week to help homeless women try to get back on their feet towards living versus merely surviving. ∎

Tiffany

Who am I?

I first came to Monterey by moving to Seaside from Modesto, CA. Now I only move around the city of Monterey. It's safer to be homeless in Monterey. There is less drug use and less trafficking. The area is nice, but it's expensive to find housing. I used to live in a nearby homeless camp, but the city had it bulldozed. They gave us twenty-four hours to get out.

My homelessness began when I lost two loved ones (men) in my live within twelve years. I slipped into a deep depression by the time 2014 came around. I have 4 kids, a bachelor's degree and a master's degree in entertainment management. I used to be a grant writer and I created business plans. My three youngest kids had to move in with my mom. My teenage daughter lived with me in my car. She was such a good kid, always with me, always worried about me because I was so vulnerable and emotionally distraught. My mom helped as much as she could, but her mobile unit could only take so many people. My daughter got help with the local Teen Safe Center. She got a job and a car and is doing well. I'm so proud of her.

I'm dealing with things better now and have the proper medicine for my depression. I also get help from a program that is helping my boyfriend and I get separate places to live. The program does not allow single couples to live together. When things settle down, my hope is to help counsel the young ones, kids around Monterey, so they don't fall victim to the streets. ▣

SIXTEEN

✙ ✙ ✙ ✙

STORIES OF TRANSFORMATION

FFERED HERE WITH permission of the individuals—whose names have also been changed

Angelina

As reported by Marisol Ramirez, Case Manager, Women in Transition, by permission of the client—whose name has been changed.

Angelina, a permanent resident of Monterey, was a long-term victim of domestic violence. Traumatized, she left her abuser and, in the absence of shelter for a homeless, unaccompanied sober woman, Angelina resorted to living in her vehicle for safety. Ultimately unable to find employment to pay for vehicle repairs and insurance, Angelina lost her vehicle and all hope for survival.

However, in December of 2015, at the age of 66, Angelina was referred to Women in Transition (WIT)

by Gathering for Women (both Fund for Homeless Women (FHW) partner programs). For the next eight months, Angelina was safely sheltered and received intensive case management services.

She received facilitated access to appropriate (physical and mental) health care, secured permanent employment and, in collaboration with Housing Resource Center's Save our Seniors (SOS) program (another FHW partner program); she obtained permanent housing with the assistance of newly obtained HUD rental subsidy.

Angelina writes (abridged):

"I will always be eternally grateful to have received the help of Community Homeless Solutions. I've undergone a great deal of trauma in my life due to abuse and homelessness, since my thirties (I'm chronologically 67 now). It's made it much harder to trust others and not be marked as a victim by those who take advantage of others.

I was blessed to find out about this wonderful organization. Thanks to their help, guidance, encouragement and focus, I've been successful in finding a home in which I believe I'll be safe and happy.

Thanks to the empathy, kindness, understanding, praise and uplifting energy of this program, I've been able to not only survive, but thrive. I've had such a hard time looking by myself, and it would get quite discouraging.

This program, and my case worker, Marisol Ramirez have truly changed my life for the better. It's very important to have a decent quality of life while you're living it. Being treated with respect and consideration, concern for our welfare and future, are completely and sincerely felt while you're in this program." ■

Helen

As reported by Marisol Ramirez, Case Manager, Women in Transition, by permission of the client—whose name has been changed.

Educated as a Medical Assistant, this forty-seven year-old unaccompanied woman worked at Walmart while living with an abusive male partner. She ultimately left her abuser, was severely traumatized and unable to afford rent. Helen lived in her vehicle for three years, during which time she developed high anxiety and could not sustain her employment.

She discovered and enrolled in the One Starfish Safe Parking Program (a Fund for Homeless Women [FHW] partner program), which then referred her to Women in Transition (also a FHW partner program)—where she was offered safe shelter, and intensive case management services.

After eighteen months, Helen could secure and maintain permanent housing and employment.

Helen writes (Abridged):

"The Women in Transition program has been a tremendous help to me. I am appreciative of the program. It has changed my life. Every step of the way, Marisol has been a great help to me. From counseling to encouragement, she helped me see a brighter light for my future.

It is with great thanks that I write this letter. I hope other women have an opportunity to enter the program. It will change their lives." ■

Ruth

As reported by Gathering for Women, by permission of the client—whose name has been changed.

"I was homeless, sleeping on the sand dunes in Monterey for a few months in 2014. I came every Tuesday to Gathering for Women" (a Fund for Homeless Women partner program) *"for food and fellowship and was so truly blessed from the help I received. The laundry vouchers were very helpful and being able to sit indoors, in peace, for even an hour or two was so appreciated at that hard time in my life. I remember being extremely*

thin and one of the volunteers helped and set aside a pair of pants for me since all the other ones were falling off. I survived in those pants for weeks.

After a few months living without shelter, I feared I would die. I just wanted to say thank you. When I was in the worst time of my life...I was very thankful for all who donated time and effort to help us women out. I know Monterey is beautiful. But the streets at night are not. So you ladies are wonderful and please know how much you help the women who are homeless."

Ruth is now working full time, paying rent, paying bills and living a great life. ∎

Holly

As reported by Roanne Wolnick, Case Manager, One Starfish Safe Parking Program by permission of the client—whose name has been changed.

"In June 2017, I met Holly. She was a vibrant, charming, enthusiastic lady who was asking for help. She had worked the past two decades working for a government agency as an Instructor in higher education. Although well respected, after speaking out about a personnel issue, which she confronted, Holly was let go from her position.

Unemployed and looking for work, Holly stayed in the homes of friends for several months. They loaned her a car and allowed her to sleep in the driveway of their homes. But that was deemed illegal and unsustainable. There were no shelters to accommodate her—unaccompanied, sober, without mental illness or yet being victimized.

Holly applied to the One Starfish Safe Parking Program (a Fund for Homeless Women partner program) in June 2017. She was safe, received case management services, immediately made friends and built community with the other clients. She continued her job search.

Soon, Holly obtained employment in downtown Monterey, where she worked in retail for about three weeks. However, she became ill and (without benefits) had to resign. When she recovered, Holly reinitiated her search and found an exciting possibility out of State.

Holly was very excited about this position and used gas cards obtained through the One Starfish program to drive to San Jose for an interview. She interviewed well, and was asked to appear for a subsequent interview out of State—which the company paid for.

She got the job. Holly left for her new life in mid-August 2017 and we were all thrilled by her determination and drive. Holly was 58 years old and still smiled as she got herself off the street, into our parking lot program and used our gas cards to find her success. ■

Lois and Wilma

As reported by Lois Varner, Program Manager, Community Church of the Monterey Peninsula, and her client, Wilma; by permission of the client (Wilma)—whose name has been changed. The lives of both have been transformed.

Through a Fund for Homeless Women grant given to the Community Church of the Monterey Peninsula, Lois (a member of the Monterey Peninsula Grand Jury) went to a community fast food restaurant to set up her program for homeless women on the Monterey Peninsula. She would arrive every week at the same time and interfaced with women who presented as homeless, living in danger and in desperate need of help. Lois listened, gave out gas cards and food coupons (which she purchased). Referrals were made to the Salvation Army for showers, and to laundromats where they could wash clothes with coupons she was able to secure.

The number of women she saw each week slowly swelled from five to fifteen to thirty-five. Ultimately, the manager of the restaurant (observing her consistency, good will and proper management of this ongoing stream of customers) offered her a permanent location in one of their booths. They even gave her extra chairs where she could meet her clients and hold conversations in an impromptu office.

Another regular customer of the restaurant noticed Lois' consistent enterprise. Although nothing bad ever happened, he became concerned about her personal safety (as the numbers continued to grow), and offered to volunteer his services as an overseer or bodyguard. Lois' case load had grown to 70 unduplicated homeless women, with 3 to 4 new cases every week.

In the meanwhile, Lois began working with the Monterey Police Department which began a distribution of blankets. She partnered with laundry facilities for jobs for the women in maintenance, doing laundry and folding clothes. Motels were collaborated with to provide employment in housekeeping; enabling women living without shelter to secure safe places to sleep, creating permanent employment and sustainable shelter.

One morning, Wilma found Lois, sitting at the fast food restaurant, as she did every week, waiting for women she could help. It was Lois who made the introduction, and over time Wilma opened up and shared her story.

Wilma had been a full-time wife and mother. She dedicated her life to caring for her husband and their severely disabled child. Recently, while struggling with grief after the death of her (then adult) child, she was abandoned by her husband—who had been the sole wage earner of the family. In her early 60's Wilma was depressed, suddenly had no income, was unable to find employment to sustain herself or pay her mortgage, and soon found herself living outside.

And the friendship, weekly mentoring, encouragement and navigation began.

Now 66 years old, with Lois' guidance and support Wilma has not only secured housing and part-time employment, but she also serves as a volunteer assistant to Lois at their pop-up program at a community fast-food restaurant. ▣

SEVENTEEN

✝ ✝ ✝ ✝

DEPRESSION

I N THE UNIVERSE OF WOMEN living without shelter with whom I became acquainted, several were
either in treatment, had been treated or were about
to be seen by a medical professional to be evaluated
for depression. In the case of the deceased, depression
was the one diagnosis (confirmed, speculated, treated or
untreated) that most shared. I wondered why?

As the National Association on Mental Illness reports,
everyone feels low sometimes, but with homelessness,
these feelings can be intense, persistent and affect the
ability to live a normal life. After all, depression is the
leading cause of disability worldwide and is a major contributor to the global burden of disease.

The most common symptoms may include feeling
sad, hopeless or anxious; loss of interest in favorite activities; feeling tired; not being able to sleep; not being able
to eat or eating too much; physical pain; and thoughts of
suicide. When I interviewed women who were homeless,

many of them described several of these symptoms. Most described them all.

Apparently, different factors play a role in the risk of depression. It can run in families. Some genetic factors increase the risk of depression. Experiences like trauma or abuse during childhood are known to raise the risk, as does trauma and stress during adulthood. Post-Traumatic Stress Disorder (PTSD) can be a major contributor. Women are two to three times more likely to develop PTSD due to stressful or traumatic experiences than men. And although not commonly listed as one of the possible life stressors and a precursor of depression, homelessness is one that should certainly be added.

In people with depression, there can be subtle changes in the brain systems involved in mood, energy, thinking and how the brain responds to stress. The changes may differ from person to person, so that a treatment that works for one may not work for another. Unfortunately, if untreated by a medical professional, many people resort to self-medicating behaviors to ease the symptoms. Over time they may develop collateral illnesses like habitual smoking, alcoholism, drug addiction or obesity.

With one in five adults in America experiencing a mental illness, it was no surprise to learn that 18 million American adults (almost 10 percent) live with clinical depression—and that only accounts for people who have been officially diagnosed. As exemplified in our population of homeless women, approximately 10.2 million adults in America eventually develop co-occurring mental health and addiction disorders.

What I (and perhaps most people) didn't realize however, is that beginning in the teen years, depression is a condition experienced more frequently by women than by men. In fact, one in eight women experience depression in their lifetime—twice the rate for men. Conversely only 40 percent of adults with a mental illness seek out or otherwise receive mental health services.

People who are homeless have food and shelter as their primary objectives. They tend to seek medical and mental health support as a last resort when faced with illness, and mostly through a hospital because of an emergency. Oftentimes, it's too late.

And when you look at the correlation between homelessness and trauma, PTSD or other anxiety disorders, it is safe to assume that many women who are homeless suffer from major depression or worse, and most suffer quietly and deeply, undiagnosed and untreated.

A warm family and healthy social connections are known to increase resilience and prevent depression, along with genetic predispositions that may increase resilience and the ability to recover from hardship. But not everyone is so fortunate.

Mental health literature advises that if a loved one is depressed, you should offer support, understanding, patience and encouragement; that you should talk to her and listen carefully; invite her out for walks, favorite activities and outings; and remind her that with time and treatment the depression will lift.

If you yourself feel depressed, you should break up large tasks into smaller ones, do what you can when you can, and do not do too many things at once. You should spend time with other people and talk to friends about your feelings; postpone important decisions until you feel better; and avoid unhealthy self-medicating activities. The experts say you should develop a new attitude, consult a professional, relax, eat well, have fun and exercise.

But we're talking about women who are homeless. Women without a voice. Women who have few friends, and less than accepting family members. Women who are traumatized, living in fear and loss, in the elements, in their vehicles or in emergency shelters, fleeing from abuse and surrounded by constant danger.

All are remarkable. Many are resilient, but how can most at some time during their homelessness avoid experiencing depression? And how can those who suffer, without appropriate medical attention, pharmacology, case management, psychological counseling, support and rapid rehousing be expected to dodge high risk for this or far greater emotional and physical ills? With prolonged homelessness, early death or severely damaged health seem almost inevitable, even for the strongest among us. And that's what I was finding in these cases.

I felt a personal responsibility and a personal connection to everyone who entrusted us with their resources, and to the homeless women we endeavor to serve. Like the women who received our support, the largest donations to the Fund were typically given anonymously. So, I didn't have the opportunity to personally thank them all. But I did thank everyone else and hoped that they came to know how much we appreciated their generosity, trust and commitment.

In time I saw that what we are attempting to tackle on the Monterey Peninsula is an infinitesimally tiny piece of a persistent global phenomenon. The historical and continued disenfranchisement and systemic social and economic injustices perpetrated against women not only result in consequences like housing insecurity and homelessness for women, but systematically bring us all down and hamper our collective progress as a people in community.

I recently heard a radio interview of an author who wrote a book about the history of psycho surgery—otherwise known as lobotomies. This author's grandfather was in fact one of the early proponents of lobotomies as surgical treatment of mental illness. In his research he discovered that women were the predominant subjects of this radical technique, most often appearing to rid these women of behaviors or characteristics that prevented them from being (what society deemed appropriate for) ideal wives. The author's own grandmother was one of the patients and lobotomized in the institution where his grandfather was the lead neurosurgeon.

I also learned of a state-of-the-art program treating adult men with autism. The program is for men only. There is no analogous program for women.

Pay and income disparities, hiring practices, ageism and sexism all continue to negatively impact women. Add power, racism, homophobia and religious intolerance to the mix, and you may get a very intense set of challenges for women to not only break through a perpetual glass ceiling, but to thrive in an often hostile living environment.

Bill and I spend quite a bit of time in Asia, mostly traveling in India. Whenever I tell someone in the U.S. where we are going they oftentimes ask, "Why are you going there? What about the poverty? What about the way they treat women?"

What about the way we treat women here? What about our poverty?

If only more of us could open our eyes and see the reality of others through a different lens, we just might see how each of us is, in some way, part of a solution. Could this broader vision cause a shift in the way we recognize our interconnectedness, and try to reimagine the ways in which we live our lives? It is not "them" and "us." It is "we." And only together are we going to be able to create sustainable change and make a lasting difference in everyone's existence. ▣

EIGHTEEN

✛ ✛ ✛ ✛

LETTING GO

ON A TRIP TO PALM SPRINGS, Bill and I woke up to a dark sky and everything covered by a thin layer of brown. It seeped inside where there was even the slightest crack and sat unnoticed on ledges and in corners until I happened upon it with clean hands or wearing white. The first time I experienced such a dust storm was in Jodhpur, India. We woke up one morning, and there it was. Like a thief in the night, the dry brown dust blew in wherever it could and laid itself down, everywhere. Piling up just inside the patio doors.

I'm not sure why, but these phantom storms came to mind as I thought about the way some people asked us to engage in policy making and political advocacy. None of us had any doubt that long term solutions for homelessness (or, simply, the availability of affordable housing) would depend on changes in public policy. Due to the growing number of our donors and the variety of folks who attended our community meetings, many recognized our potential influence on political will and encouraged us to actively participate in the process.

I didn't consider it mission creep. I'd already been vocal about wondering if we should assume leadership to create or encourage an advocacy arm whose mission would be to focus on public policy, educate the community about policy issues that affect homeless women, inform us about civic meetings, the status of ordinances and policy changes, and encourage coordinated positions that the Fund could publicly articulate. We couldn't come to consensus, and so it did not become a clearly defined aspect of our work. But it could, and perhaps to some degree in the future, it will.

In the meanwhile I wrote letters to the editor, attended and spoke at city council meetings, encouraged political leaders to attend our public gatherings and in many ways brought them to engage in our cause. My amigos and I had made it a point to remain politically impartial. We are a fund, not a political action committee. We want more housing for the homeless, and in realizing that our donor base represented a broad political spectrum, did not want to get caught up in any political ideology. But how could we come to exert more influence in policy making and become more effective advocates for women who are homeless? This is a question that has become more relevant as we continue to grow.

And there was also the question of energy. Kathy, Marian and I were senior citizens. Because I was the youngest, I tended to represent the Fund at most policy related events. But most of our meetings took place in the evening, and seemed to become more numerous and contentious. Kathy attended most daytime meetings and seemed to be saying, "I'm old!" with greater frequency. Maybe that's where the dust is coming from—age. Cobwebs or rust might also be an appropriate metaphor. Whatever I did, or didn't do, I just couldn't seem to get away from the dust.

I not too secretly longed for the time when I would feel in total control of my time. There I was, for all intents and purposes, considered to be retired and I still oftentimes felt overwhelmed with commitments, and being over scheduled. I no longer enjoyed running from appointment to appointment, would rather not feel guilty for having to cancel because I suddenly planned a trip or just didn't feel like being responsible, as I had for so much of my life.

I came to the realization that I needed to decide for myself when enough would be enough. When I would feel as if I had accomplished what I had set out to do. When it was time to stop. When it was time to move on. It's quite an interesting question. As I look back, some endings appeared to happen slowly, during a long process of discovery. Others seemed to occur suddenly. But ultimately, I felt like in each case I made the right decision, without regret.

It was clear to me when it was time to leave parish ministry. I got up one morning while on retreat, and I heard a voice, literally. And it felt as if a tremendous load had been taken off my shoulder. It was clear to me as when it was time to leave my first marriage. Enough was very clear to me then as well.

Earlier in my life, better jobs and greater income made moving to the next thing easy and practical. But this feels very different. Endings now are like markers in a finite life, the likes of which grow less likely to be repeated, as I move closer to the ultimate. It signifies aging and diminishment, a life getting smaller.

Although I sense its approach, the end of my work in this ministry is still some ways off. In the meantime I feel the need to be measured in the things I commit myself to—the meetings, committees, speaking engagements, projects and responsibilities I assume.

When would enough be enough? It wasn't clear. I was sure it would be clear later, when it finally was. However, like dust in a storm, everywhere I went, without even trying, I saw women who were homeless. I seemed to be somehow drawn to them.

As I walked to church in Palm Springs I spotted two women who were clearly living outside. I didn't want to see them or remember that feeling of helplessness always lying in wait at the pit of my stomach. But there they were. *Visible.*

One woman dragged a large bag like a stubborn child, as she examined trash on the street. Gray dominated her dry and brittle silhouette. Another struggled with her belongings, walking barefoot on the hot pavement, her back covered in blisters from the 105 degree sun. This too is America. What do I do? What do I say? Even I continued to ask myself those questions.

Eyes and outstretched hands appear to me in dark corners like apparitions, emerging from behind dumpsters, driving up in cars packed to overflowing with belongings, or blocking me on the sidewalk with sun-baked arms laden with bursting bags. Even the ones trying to be less obvious, trying not to be seen or picked out in a crowd, wanting to blend in, wanting to belong, seemed to look deep into my soul—disturbing its failing attempts to be at rest.

And the women standing behind the counter, pushing a broom, bussing my table; I wonder where she slept the night before. Does she have a safe place to stay tonight? Did she sleep in her car? Did she take a shower in the park? Who caused that bruise on her face? Were there wounds hiding beneath her clothes?

Over time it became a sort of obsession. There were so many. I didn't want to get too close. I didn't want to ask. After all I didn't have the answer. I didn't have what they needed. I didn't always have a place for them to go. And I always felt as if I should. The stubborn assumption of many in Monterey and all over the country was that there was a safe place, a solution, a shelter in paradise somewhere to accommodate all who required it. I must know where that is. But in reality it didn't always exist.

Although much less than in months past, my phone still rings with calls from women who need a place to spend the night, or from friends of women who are homeless or struggling on the brink. There always seems to be a message waiting for my attention. A message from a woman asking for help.

I share the resources that I have, the names and contact information of service providers I know, the ones we had helped create and proudly support, but it's often not enough. It's never enough, really and I quite often felt that I had failed. It was so much easier when I just couldn't see.

Grief and loss are part of the human condition. My heart had been broken before, and healing from one break invariably led to yet another cycle of psychic pain. I even ended up in the hospital from this all too common malady. I had experienced the longest bout of atrial fibrillation—almost continuously starting Thursday after the presidential elections. Hillary Clinton was defeated by Donald Trump.

I took medication, meditated, prayed and tried to sleep but it continued until I was dizzy, breathless and weak. What frightened me the most was a sense of confusion and a sudden lack of mental clarity. When I broke into tears for no apparent reason, I knew that I needed to seek medical attention. Bill took me to the emergency room.

While on the gurney, I returned to sinus rhythm, a full breath, oxygenation and sound mind. It was determined that I didn't have a heart attack or stroke (as was initially assumed), but taking as much beta blocker as I had in the past twenty-four hours reduced my blood pressure and significantly compromised alertness.

I'll never know conclusively if the election results were the cause of my condition. But I did wonder if doctors around the country (particularly in blue states) would see an uptick in office visits for issues triggered by politics. The question would probably emerge as a popular research project for theses in 2017.

Physical illnesses related to trauma, fear, anger and anxiety are real and seemed inevitable for those of us who felt personally affected by the rhetoric and unfortunate discord that had been perpetrated throughout the presidential campaign—characteristics I perceived Trump had emblazoned, personified, and was now building an administration to advance. I knew the election results were having a deep emotional impact on me, but I didn't realize how much, how deep. My grief was pervasive and lasted for weeks, hanging in the air, even as I write these words.

I also didn't realize how much I was being affected by the transition we were facing in the Fund. As we completed annual grantmaking decisions at the Community Foundation for our fourth round of awards, I did all I could to hold back tears. Not only was I saddened by the fact that we couldn't provide as much support as we wanted, but since we were transitioning to endowment fundraising, we thought we would be giving away even less money for several years to come.

While we agreed to remain active in community building, public awareness and advocacy; we also decided to inform our grantees of a shift toward endowment building, so that they could prepare their budgets and fundraising plans accordingly.

Even more impactful than that however, was seeing the programs we helped to start, now building infrastructure. They were growing their capacity and moving forward, while also continuing to deplete the number of our donors and financial backers.

In one sense their success was a very good thing. It was consolation and exactly what we had hoped for. But how could we be expected to be there with generous annual support, while being stripped of our resources? This conundrum should have been viewed as a natural organizational transition, but crossing what I experienced as a chasm simply overwhelmed me.

There was a large front-page article in the newspaper about the assessment of the status of women who are homeless on the Monterey Peninsula, which we had commissioned through the Community Foundation. Nowhere in the article was there mention of the Fund for Homeless Women. Rather there were several direct quotes from Gathering for Women board members.

Riding on the power of our assessment, the article turned out to be an awesome marketing opportunity for their program. Had I not already done so, I would have written them a check myself.

When I arrived at my Zumba class later that day, several people had seen the article and congratulated me. Another class member informed me of a major gift to the Gathering for Women he and his wife had made in my honor. And later that evening, I received an email from a friend informing me that the Berkeley Museum of Art recently bought a drawing she had done of me, and she donated her entire commission from the sale in my honor to (you guessed it) the Gathering for Women.

All good, but as our "baby" organizations ramped up their own fundraising, donations to the Fund were getting smaller in size and less frequent. Had we already peaked? As we alluded to before, we would certainly have to change our strategy, adjust our messaging and be more assertive in our own fundraising practices, being careful to avoid the appearance of competition. Wanting to have significant resources for the Fund's viability and usefulness in providing housing and other services for women in the future, we would have to be more robust in campaigning, and more direct in soliciting new donors.

After only five years of operation, we would now have to reimagine our purpose, retool our goals and reshape the language we used to communicate our objectives. It would also necessitate an infusion of enthusiasm.

Evolution takes time and energy. I felt devoid of both, along with the absence of motivation to carry on. Grief does that. In spite of what we had achieved, I felt crestfallen and was only able to see the glass half empty, focusing on loss and all that was left undone.

I thought back to the occasion of saying good bye to my daughter when she started college. I stood on the steps of her dorm, teary-eyed and in a bundle of emotions. She was on the precipice of a new chapter in her young life, successfully embarking on a new journey. She was leaving the nest with wings, and from a launching pad that I helped create as a single parent in Los Angeles. But standing amid all the excitement and chaos, the sadness I felt was real. There would be no turning back. We had crossed a significant and complex threshold. And it hurt.

Social entrepreneurs want the things we help shape to move on, to grow and flourish. Parents want their children to become independent, to individuate and go off on their own. But it's painful when they leave. It changes our identity and for a while, we feel lost and left behind. It's a heart thing. It doesn't make sense, we should know better but the sadness we feel is real.

That's how it was for me at the end of making our grant decisions in 2016. I felt broken hearted, inadequate and left behind; having lost sight of all that we had accomplished. But life was moving on and I needed to let go once again. ▣

NINETEEN

✛ ✛ ✛ ✛

SHAME

HAD A SPEAKING ENGAGEMENT with another Rotary Club, this time in Salinas. It was enjoyable, and I believe time well spent. There were roughly thirty people in attendance, all very interested and informed—a different dynamic than what I've grown accustomed to at these speaking engagements. Everyone seemed very savvy. Most were involved with the current developments of a program called Dorothy's Kitchen in Salinas, including the board chair of Dorothy's, who gave a report on their new showers and health center. No one would have believed that in just a few months later, their shelter program for women would temporarily have to close.

I was presented with a $500 check made out to the One Starfish Safe Parking Program (a program the Fund helped start). I told the member who invited me to speak, that she owed me one "for the Fund." We laughed. She reminded me that she and her husband had come to the very first speaking engagement Kathy and I gave at the

Carmel Valley Public Library. They had supported us from the very beginning, and were well-aware of our evolution and unique challenges.

The club members were appreciative and complementary. They encouraged us to continue our "very wise" strategy of assessment and broad-based investment, but were especially impressed by our attention to planning and endowment fundraising. It was enjoyable to talk to a group that understood. And the chicken dinner was actually quite good.

On the heels of that meeting came another that at first felt disappointing. As I sat there, I wondered if I should have turned down this invitation to speak on a panel for the local ACLU. I wasn't sure if the right message was being delivered, or if the right message was being received. Luckily there weren't many people in the audience.

The keynote was someone from Fresno who wrote a book about his work with the homeless. Besides assisting with lawsuits, which ultimately stopped the removal and destruction of personal property in encampments, he provided porta-potties and garbage receptacles where homeless people gathered. He also helped facilitate conversations and a community response to the homeless in his area. It was clear that he walked the talk. He was aware of the complexity and the nuance. I believed his story. He was doing his part.

On the dais was a homeless advocate from Tulare. Tia Sukin from the One Starfish Safe Parking Program was there and me. Maybe I'm projecting, but despite my best efforts to offer something new, it sounded like the same old thing. It couldn't possibly have been interesting to the folks in the audience. It wasn't even interesting to me. They all looked bored, tired or just overwhelmed. And that evening, so was I.

After we all spoke, the moderator asked the audience for input: "Have you looked into Fort Ord?" someone asked. "Have you thought about Tiny Houses?" shouted another. Someone else said that we should all march on City Hall, and not forget to tell stories. Someone shouted. "Nothing works better than telling stories." Another suggested, "You should go to city council meetings and take hundreds of people along with you." "And don't forget to tell stories!" the now familiar voice said once again.

It was after 8:00 in the evening, and I was getting a bit weary.

To change the dynamic, I asked the moderator if I could ask the audience a question. She said yes, and so I asked them where their friends were. I asked them why the room wasn't packed. Why there wasn't an outrage? Why weren't we turning people away for lack of room, because there were so many others who recognized that we were in fact looking at a crisis, and that the urgency for addressing the needs of the poor and homeless was at an all-time high, and getting worse?

I asked them why every chair wasn't filled with people who were deeply disturbed by the fact that women were living and dying on the streets of the peninsula because the homeless had few, if any options for safety and shelter, right here, in this place we call paradise? I asked them where everybody was, and why wasn't everyone else mad as hell.

The room fell quiet and I realized I must have done something terribly wrong. But at least I woke myself up. And I seemed to have provoked at least one other person who raised her hand and acknowledged the awkward silence.

She challenged her fellow audience members to think about what I had asked, and later, as I walked out the door to go home, she stopped me and went on to talk about shame.

She said that she had been thinking about shame and empathy for a long time, and had pondered why it seems to be so much easier to raise money for animal rescue than it was to rescue human beings. Why instead of Pet of the Week, on the evening news, didn't we have Person of the Week? I wondered as well.

She said she had always noticed that the reaction to seeing a lost dog was always more immediate and empathetic than when encountering a person who was homeless. The former typically arouses sympathy and engagement, while the latter most often results in displeasure and avoidance.

She thought it had a lot to do with shame. That we experience shame when we have a close encounter with another person in desperation or need, particularly if they are unpleasant to look at. Shame, because she is in that condition. Shame, because we may have been complicit in her becoming what she is. Shame, because of feeling helpless, not knowing what to do, not doing enough or anything at all.

Of course, there's also indifference, annoyance and even anger. When encountering the homeless many passers-by create the narrative that the homeless person obviously made the wrong life choices, just didn't work hard enough. Perhaps she is enjoying drugs or alcohol, wishes to be living as they are or is lazy, dishonest and simply scamming the system.

But shame in the giver and the housed, asking them for help? I hadn't considered it as a possible barrier to empathy or to an impediment to imagining solutions, of creating pathways to making a difference, or at least attempting to help change the lives of others.

Certainly we can imagine shame on the part of the homeless, and from the effects of trauma, from living outside. But shame on the part of those who are sheltered and safe, our collective shame, was a new concept that made my time with the ACLU well worth it.

This woman, whose name I never learned, told me that she was a communications specialist and suggested that to continue building a response for systemic change, we might find ways for people to work through their shame, like the victims of war or violence who must first work through trauma before being able to access sustainable treatment and assimilate the kind of care that transforms. Or professionals who do diversity training, starting first with exploring the participants own experiences of racism, power and privilege that they may have personally perpetrated, been complicit or even apathetic.

She said she would call me to talk about this further but asked me to begin to think of ways to get people to have focused conversations about the homeless, to create safe spaces where people could just talk and listen, and if they could get deeper, to reveal and explore their shame. "It's there," she said, "just waiting to be discovered."

Shame. Could that be why for so long, I couldn't even see it? Could it be the blinders for us all? ▣

TWENTY

✛ ✛ ✛ ✛

THE STORY CONTINUES

AN ARTICLE IN THE NEWSPAPER caught me by surprise. Apparently, a narrative for the woman whose body was most recently found in Carmel was being developed. I had been unable to learn anything about her for several months since her identification had been undetermined and the investigation was ongoing.

But on November 1, 2016, there was a brief flash on the evening news and an article in the morning paper announcing that her identification had been established. As suspected, she was homeless. The cause and circumstances related to her death had not been determined but there was hope that by making her name public, someone would come forward with information that would help the County Sheriff's office with their investigation.

Her name was Remie Casillas. The article noted that she was not local. She came from neighboring Santa Cruz (a fact that most people in Monterey seemed to remember more readily than her actual name). It would take time for us to learn more about her story, if, in fact, we ever would. ▣

EPILOGUE

✛ ✛ ✛ ✛

THE STATE OF CALIFORNIA passed a law (Senate Bill 1069 and Assembly Bill 2299, Statutes of 2016) requiring all cities to allow the rental of second units to ease the lack of affordable housing in their jurisdictions. This would not legitimize Airbnb rentals or short-term rentals less than thirty days, but was indeed surprising since the prohibition of this practice had been passionately argued during a recent City Council meeting. Many claimed that allowing the legalization of second unit rentals would ruin the character of their great city.

Now it seemed as if the city would have no choice but to allow it. The caveat may be that the city would be able to determine exactly where (and only where) within the jurisdiction this would be allowed. Wherever they ultimately choose, if implemented as intended, this might help provide additional affordable housing stock in our very shallow pool of inventory.

Additionally, an advisory committee agreed with Monterey County housing and planning staff that an upcoming subdivision called Rancho Canada Village would be required to meet the letter of the law on the county's inclusionary housing rules—also to be debated by the Council and Planning Commission in the upcoming weeks. Breaking long held tradition, the committee agreed that county code would require the 130 lot housing project to include a mix of 26 very low-income, low income and moderate income affordable housing units in order to meet its inclusionary housing obligation.

In spite of the existence of this (20 percent) code, the developer proposed to build 25 medium income rental townhomes to meet the obligation and/or (as developers in our county had been able to do successfully in the past) buy itself out of the requirement. However, the committee agreed that this time the developer would be required to build affordable units on site rather than pay an in-lieu fee.

With the legalization of second units and the completion of MIDPEN and CHISPA building projects, inventory of affordable housing in our county should increase significantly over the coming years. The policy tide that ruled our civic lives seemed suddenly to be shifting.

To add to this newly found optimism, Marian brought to our attention the passage of Proposition HHH in Southern California and suggested we consider attempting a similar policy action for Monterey County.

According to the *LA Times,* Los Angeles voters widely favored an ambitious bond measure to pay for homeless and affordable housing in their city. The proposition would raise $1.2 billion to create between 8,000 and 10,000 permanent supportive housing units for the city's homeless, as well as facilities for access to mental health counseling, addiction services and housing placement.

Proposition HHH garnered the support of about 76 percent of votes cast. It needed 66.67 percent to pass. Data from the Los Angeles Homeless Services Authority indicated 28,000 homeless men, women and children are living in the City of Angels. One-tenth of Los Angeles' population lives in Monterey County. But in both locations, the issue has been aggravated by a lack of affordable housing, low vacancy rates and rising rents. Why couldn't we hope to achieve the same or more with votes here, in paradise?

Under the measure, the city would borrow money by issuing general obligation bonds and pay off the debt with a new property tax on commercial and residential properties. The LA tax would last for nearly three decades and would fluctuate, depending on the amount of money needed for housing each year. Over the life of the bonds, a property owner would pay an estimated average annual tax rate of $9.64 for every $100,000 of assessed valuation.

Why couldn't we consider working on something like this for Monterey County? It would certainly be worth considering.

And most recently, the Monterey County Board of Supervisors took a bold step and passed two initiatives for the homeless. Supervisors recognized homelessness in the county as an emergency, and agreed to allocate $850,000 for the One Starfish Safe Parking Program to expend its parking program (currently supported by the Fund for Women), and for Community Homeless Solutions (also supported by the Fund) to operate a winter warming Shelter. These are courageous steps toward housing diversity for a fair and thriving community where no one gets left behind.

Dedicated to shelter, safety and community, the Fund for Homeless Women is here to stay. After all, many claim we live in paradise. And, in paradise, there's always more than enough to go around. ▣

ABOUT THE AUTHOR

✛ ✛ ✛ ✛

MICHAEL E. REID, a retired Episcopal priest, has published three collections of personal essays, *My Own Skin; Searching for Home; Grand Illusions: The Making of a 21st Century Man* (2011). Other works have been published in *Life in Pacific Grove* (2017), *The LLI Review* (Fall 2011), *CURE* (Summer 2010) and in the Community Foundation for Monterey County blog. Reid received an EdD from Temple University and an MDiv from the Church Divinity School of the Pacific. He currently resides in Monterey, California. ▣

OTHER BOOKS BY 2LEAF PRESS

2Leaf Press challenges the status quo by publishing alternative fiction, non-fiction, poetry and bilingual works by activists, academics, poets and authors dedicated to diversity and social justice with scholarship that is accessible to the general public. 2Leaf Press produces high quality and beautifully produced hardcover, paperback and ebook formats through our series: 2LP Explorations in Diversity, 2LP University Books, 2LP Classics, 2LP Translations, Nuyorican World Series, and 2LP Current Affairs, Culture & Politics. Below is a selection of 2Leaf Press' published titles.

2LP EXPLORATIONS IN DIVERSITY

Substance of Fire: Gender and Race in the College Classroom
by Claire Millikin
Foreword by R. Joseph Rodríguez, Afterword by Richard Delgado
Contributors Riley Blanks, Blake Calhoun, Rox Trujillo

Black Lives Have Always Mattered
A Collection of Essays, Poems, and Personal Narratives
Edited by Abiodun Oyewole

The Beiging of America:
Personal Narratives about Being Mixed Race in the 21st Century
Edited by Cathy J. Schlund-Vials, Sean Frederick Forbes, Tara Betts
with an Afterword by Heidi Durrow

What Does it Mean to be White in America?
Breaking the White Code of Silence, A Collection of Personal Narratives
Edited by Gabrielle David and Sean Frederick Forbes
Introduction by Debby Irving and Afterword by Tara Betts

2LP UNIVERSITY BOOKS
Designs of Blackness
Mappings in the Literature and Culture of African Americans
by A. Robert Lee
20TH ANNIVERSARY EXPANDED EDITION

2LP CLASSICS
Adventures in Black and White
by Philippa Schuyler
Edited and with a critical introduction by Tara Betts

Monsters: Mary Shelley's Frankenstein and Mathilda
by Mary Shelley, edited by Claire Millikin Raymond

2LP TRANSLATIONS
Birds on the Kiswar Tree
by Odi Gonzales, Translated by Lynn Levin
Bilingual: English/Spanish

Incessant Beauty, A Bilingual Anthology
by Ana Rossetti, Edited and Translated by Carmela Ferradáns
Bilingual: English/Spanish

NUYORICAN WORLD SERIES
Our Nuyorican Thing, The Birth of a Self-Made Identity
by Samuel Carrion Diaz, with an Introduction by Urayoán Noel
Bilingual: English/Spanish

Hey Yo! Yo Soy!, 40 Years of Nuyorican Street Poetry,
The Collected Works of Jesús Papoleto Meléndez
Bilingual: English/Spanish

LITERARY NONFICTION
No Vacancy; Homeless Women in Paradise
by Michael Reid

The Beauty of Being, A Collection of Fables, Short Stories & Essays
by Abiodun Oyewole

WHEREABOUTS: Stepping Out of Place,
An Outside in Literary & Travel Magazine Anthology
Edited by Brandi Dawn Henderson

PLAYS
Rivers of Women, The Play
by Shirley Bradley LeFlore, with photographs by Michael J. Bracey

AUTOBIOGRAPHIES/MEMOIRS/BIOGRAPHIES
Trailblazers, Black Women Who Helped Make America Great
American Firsts/American Icons
by Gabrielle David
Edited by Carolina Fung Feng

Mother of Orphans
The True and Curious Story of Irish Alice, A Colored Man's Widow
by Dedria Humphries Barker

Strength of Soul
by Naomi Raquel Enright

Dream of the Water Children:
Memory and Mourning in the Black Pacific
by Fredrick D. Kakinami Cloyd
Foreword by Velina Hasu Houston, Introduction by Gerald Horne
Edited by Karen Chau

The Fourth Moment: Journeys from the Known to the Unknown, A Memoir
by Carole J. Garrison, Introduction by Sarah Willis

POETRY
PAPOLíTICO, Poems of a Political Persuasion
by Jesús Papoleto Meléndez
with an Introduction by Joel Kovel and DeeDee Halleck

Critics of Mystery Marvel, Collected Poems
by Youssef Alaoui, with an Introduction by Laila Halaby

shrimp
by jason vasser-elong, with an Introduction by Michael Castro

The Revlon Slough, New and Selected Poems
by Ray DiZazzo, with an Introduction by Claire Millikin

Written Eye: Visuals/Verse
by A. Robert Lee

A Country Without Borders: Poems and Stories of Kashmir
by Lalita Pandit Hogan, with an Introduction by Frederick Luis Aldama

Branches of the Tree of Life
The Collected Poems of Abiodun Oyewole 1969-2013
by Abiodun Oyewole, edited by Gabrielle David
with an Introduction by Betty J. Dopson

2Leaf Press is an imprint owned and operated by the Intercultural Alliance of Artists & Scholars, Inc. (IAAS), a NY-based nonprofit organization that publishes and promotes multicultural literature.

NEW YORK
www.2leafpress.org